MW00637272

# Search of the Soul

## 15 SMALL GROUP STUDIES
### ON FINDING PEACE WITH GOD

DISCOVERY SERIES

## KELLY PEAVEY
## LAUREL EDISON
## LORRAINE MULLIGAN DAVIS

David C. Cook Publishing Co.
Colorado Springs, CO/Paris, Ontario

This Leader's Guide is the companion to the *Search of the Soul Journal* in the *Great Groups Discovery Series*, a home Bible study series for high school through young adults. Appropriate both for Christians and seekers, it sheds light on the Bible's answers to questions about our search for God.

GREAT GROUPS
Discovery Series
**Search of the Soul Leader's Guide**
© 1995 David C. Cook Publishing Co. All rights reserved.

No part of this book may be reproduced in any form without the written permission of the publisher, unless otherwise stated in the text.

Unless otherwise noted, Scripture quotations are from the Holy Bible, New International Version (NIV), © 1973, 1978, 1984 by International Bible Society. Used by permission of Zondervan Bible Publishers.

Published by David C. Cook Church Ministry Resources,
a division of Cook Communications Ministries International
Colorado Springs, CO 80918
Cable address: DCCOOK
Editor: Sue Reck. Contributors: Kelly Peavey, Laurel Edison, Lorraine Mulligan Davis.
Designer: Jeff Sharpton, PAZ Design. Cover illustrator: Ken Cuffe.
Inside illustrator: Jim Carson.
Printed in U.S.A. ISBN: 0-7814-5201-5

# TABLE OF Contents

# Schedule

| Meeting | Date | Location | Leaders | Helpers (food, etc.) |
|---|---|---|---|---|

**Optional Meeting**

**Searchers One and All**

1

2

3

4

5

**What I'm Searching For**

6

7

8

9

10

**The End of the Search, The Beginning of a Journey**

11

12

13

14

15

# Great Stuff about *Great Groups!*

Welcome to *Great Groups*—a new concept in youth ministry resources from David C. Cook. *Great Groups* is a three-tiered series of studies created for high schoolers and young adults who are at various stages of spiritual development. The three tiers—designed to move young people from being casual about Christianity to becoming committed followers of Jesus Christ—look like this:

**Spiritual Maturity**    **Focus**

Committed    The Main Thing    Discipleship

Curious    The Good Word    Bible Study

Casual    Discovery Series    Human Need

*Great Groups* **was created because:**

• Not all young people are at the same stage of spiritual development;

• Intentional ministry is needed to guide people toward greater spiritual commitment;

• Real life change is possible through studying the Bible individually and discussing it together in small groups;

• Many young people are ready to lead discussion groups, so these studies encourage peer leadership;

• No two small groups are the same, so these studies pay attention to group dynamics.

*The Discovery Series*—Entry-level studies for seekers and those who've grown up in the church, but who may not have a complete understanding of what it means to be a Christian. These studies help people discover who they are from God's perspective, and the difference that can make in every area of their lives. The *Discovery Series* assumes group members have little or no Bible background. Minimal advance preparation needed.

*The Good Word Series*—Inductive studies for those who are curious about what the Bible really says. These studies help young people develop lifelong Bible study skills that will challenge them to feed themselves from Scripture. *The Good Word Series* assumes group members have little or some Bible background. Moderate advance preparation needed.

*The Main Thing Series*—Discipleship studies for those who want to be followers of Jesus Christ. These studies will challenge group members to take their faith seriously. *The Main Thing Series* assumes group members have some or extensive Bible background. Thorough advance preparation needed.

# How to Use This Material

## Why a Small Group Bible Study?

"No man is an island," said English poet John Donne. The search for identity is a personal search, but the irony is that it can never be discovered only on one's own. That is the reason for exploring the question in a small group setting. In your journal you can explore your own thinking and reflect and express your thoughts and feelings, always with reference to something greater than yourself—the Word of God. The small group should be a safe place to explore those things with others. In a sense, when you express something personal in a group, you do a reality check. The group members either affirm or correct your impression by their reactions, and you do the same for them. Sometimes that's painful; sometimes it's wonderfully affirming. The important thing is to be sensitive, to respect and listen to one another, and to be gentle with one another.

Throughout this guide, there will be suggestions for activities and questions to help build a sense of community in which true discovery can take place.

## Digging In: Studying the Bible Inductively

You do not have to *believe* the Bible to study it inductively. All that's required is an openness to letting the text speak for itself. Inductive means you go from the particular—in this case, the text in front of you—to the general—what you can learn from it.

The role of the leader in an inductive study is to ask questions and guide the group members into the text to dig out the meaning for themselves, rather than telling them what it means. The leader is not the expert. In fact, anyone can lead.

Studying the Bible requires adherence to the same rules you would use in interpreting any body of literature. But first, a ground rule: The *text* is the authority, not something you heard in a sermon or something you read in a book (though these can be helpful). Stick to the passage under discussion and let it speak for itself.

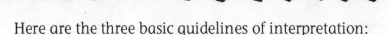

Here are the three basic guidelines of interpretation:

**1. What does the passage say? (Observation.)** Answering this involves the "5 Ws and 1 H" of journalism:

- *Who* is writing or speaking, and to whom? *Who* are the people involved?

- *What* kind of writing is it? (Letter? Poem? Historical account? Narrative? Prophecy?) *What* parts can we see? *What* was the writer's train of thought? *What* are the author's tactics? *What* is happening?

- *Where* is the action taking place? (What country? At whose house? What does the setting tell you?)

- *When* is all of this happening? This does not mean simply a date or year (unless the text says so). It means at what point in Jesus' ministry, or after what and before what other events in the Bible, or at what time of day—whatever the text itself *says* about time.

- *Why?* Does one event or person cause something else to happen? *What* are the motives and feelings? *Why* did the author write this? Is he persuading, reporting, worshiping, teaching?

- *How* does each part relate to the whole? *How* is the story or argument being told or arranged?

**2. What does it mean? (Interpretation.)** Only when you've analyzed the text to find out what it actually says can you seek to answer the question "What does it mean?" This is where most problems of interpretation come in. Sometimes there are layers of interpretation, but usually there is one basic meaning of the text—at least for the time in which it was written. This, of course, does not mean that you will like what it says, but if the text is allowed to speak for itself, rather than having us impose the meaning we want on it, we can accept or reject it with integrity.

To discover the meaning of the text, ask questions such as these: How does the style affect our interpretation? Did the writer intend for this to be taken literally, or is it a story with a moral to it, such as the parables of Jesus? There are legitimate differences of interpretation on some passages, but discovering the writer's intent eliminates many, if not, most different meanings.

**3. What does it mean to me? (Application.)** Too often people jump right to this question the first time they read a passage. Ideally, this is the last question you should answer. Only when the first two questions are answered can you

legitimately ask what the passage means to you specifically, and to people in general.

The Holy Spirit is ultimately the interpreter of God's Word to our hearts, and you don't have to be a scholar to understand and "hear" God speaking to you through a verse or passage of Scripture. But by jumping to this question without really understanding what the text actually says and what it means, you can come up with errors and weird interpretations.

## Sharing the Leadership

This series is designed to be led by participants. The leader doesn't have to be an expert (the text is, remember?). Most sessions have leadership tips to help you in your role as leader. Basically, the leader's role is to ask questions and guide the group in discovery. You might want to rotate the leadership so that everyone has a chance to lead. If some people don't want to lead a study, that's OK. Start off with someone who's led a Bible study before, go for a few weeks, and then hand off the leadership to someone else.

The leader's job is to facilitate discussion. Do not allow anyone—not even yourself—to monopolize the discussion. Try to draw out more reserved members, but don't force anyone to talk who doesn't want to. Give people time to think and don't be afraid of a little silence.

If someone comes up with an "off the wall" interpretation, ask something like, "Where do you see that meaning in the text?" Sometimes the group corrects itself. Someone might wonder about the comment and say what he or she sees in the verses. Or you could ask other people what they think—as long as they stick with the text too.

If someone brings up something that's off the subject of the text, say so, but offer to follow up on it later. Don't let the group get sidetracked into an argument. If there's a legitimate disagreement, let people express their points, and then say, "Let's move on; we can discuss this later," or even, "We probably have to agree to disagree about this, but let's continue with the study."

## What Version of the Bible Should We Use?

This really doesn't matter, but whatever you use, it's a good idea for everyone to use the same version of Scripture. You may want to have an alternate trans-

lation along for comparison purposes, but you'll avoid confusion if everyone is reading the same text. Another value in using the same translation (in the same edition) is that you can tell people what page to turn to for those who don't yet know how to find books in the Bible.

Most of the Scripture printed in the journal is in the New International Version (NIV) of the Bible. This is a good modern translation. If you want to use the NIV, you can order inexpensive paperback versions from the International Bible Society.

# The Format

These studies are broken down into three five-week units. As a group, decide how you will approach this material. These units build on each other, so it's ideal if you have fifteen weeks to go through them all in order, with perhaps a break in between units. Do at least make an initial five-week commitment, and then you can reevaluate.

Another group decision is how much time you'll spend together for each study. The study can easily be done in an hour to an hour and a half. Two hours together will give you time for refreshments afterward. Be sure to allow at least 30 minutes for the study itself and 5-10 minutes for actual prayer at the end, and not just the sharing of requests. Also, make sure that it's understood exactly when your study is going to start. Always start at the same time to ensure commitment. Here's an outline of the format with suggested time limits for each part.

# 1 Getting Started (15-20 minutes)

One of the most important parts of your time together. You can use this time to welcome new people, help people get to know each other, and move into a frame of mind to discuss the topic of the week.

## Housekeeping (3-5 minutes)

This is the place for announcements (for example, a change in the meeting location, a schedule change, or plans for a social activity outside of group time). Keep these short and sweet.

## Icebreaker (5-10 minutes)

A mixer or getting-to-know-you activity to help people feel that the group is a safe place for sharing nonthreatening things.

## Opening (5 minutes)

This is a transition activity to open yourselves to God and invite His Presence through singing, prayer, or other creative devotional activity.

# 2 Bible Study (30-45 minutes)

## Focus (about 5 minutes)

This brief, introductory section should be an activity or question that shows the relevance of today's study to people's lives. Sometimes, the question or activity will relate to something in the journals, so it's a good idea for people to bring them every week.

## Dig In (20-30 minutes)

This is the heart of your study. In this section, the goal of the leader is to move the group through the observation and interpretation process. Study the passage for yourself before you look at this guide; make notes of the questions and ideas you come up with. Then choose from the questions or ideas suggested here. We will sometimes include "Inside Insights," notes to help you understand the passage better.

## Reflect and Respond (5-10 minutes)

This brief section is very important. It's here that you ask the "so what?" questions of application. "How did this study help me, challenge me, relate to my life?" "What will I do as a result of this, or how has my perspective changed?" Frequently this will be a chance for people to share something from their journals. Sometimes, too, this will be a time for members to do something expressive to show what they got out of the study.

# 3 Sharing and Prayer (15-25 minutes)

Here's the time where you allow people to talk about what's going on in their lives and pray for one another. You can leave this totally open-ended, or you can use this time to talk more about your journals. Make sure that you actually spend some time (5-10 minutes at least) in prayer and that you don't just talk about yourselves until it's time to go home. Use the section at the back of the journals to record prayer requests and praises.

# Come Now, Let Us Reason Together

**Theme:** Introductory meeting. If you haven't used the *Discovery Series* before, consider starting with this. It will provide a general introduction to the group, introduce the Discovery Bible study series concept and the journal, and give you the opportunity to make a covenant to explore the Bible's answers to these questions together.

**Scripture:** Isaiah 1:1-20

# 1 Getting Started (15-20 minutes)

## Icebreaker

Here are a couple of mixer ideas. The first one's good for learning names, the second for getting to know each other. (Both were taken from *Incredible Meeting Makers: Mix it Up!*, David C. Cook.)

### Sentence Sharing

Everyone will need a pencil and paper. Have each person write the first initial of each group member's first name down the left-hand side of the paper—start-

ing with his or her own name and continuing clockwise around the group. Next, have each person make a sentence out of all of the letters, with each initial being the first letter of each word in the sentence. The sentences must make sense and may not use any of the participants' full names. If people can't make their sentences work, let them rearrange themselves and start over. When they have finished, they should read their acrostic sentences to the rest of the group.

## A & Q

Before the session, get some small, square boxes or cube-shaped wooden blocks that can be held in one hand. Tape or glue a label on each side of each box or block. Write the following on the labels (one phrase per label):

a. Yes, but I'll never do that again.

b. Because I was curious.

c. Yes, and I'd do it again if I could.

d. No, and I never would.

e. Because my parents told me to.

f. Yes, but I don't know why.

Explain that people will take turns rolling the cube to see which answer comes up. After rolling the cube, a person must come up with a question that goes with the answer on the cube. For example, a person who rolled the answer, "Because I was curious," might come up with a question like, "Why did I stick my finger in a light socket when I was three?"

Questions must be based on real events in the person's life. Play as many rounds as you have time for.

If you don't have time to tape labels on cubes, simply write the answers on a large sheet of paper, numbered one through six, and have group members roll dice instead of cubes.

## Housekeeping (Today this will take up a larger share of your time.)

Take a break from any goofiness (and allow for the inevitable late-comer) by making necessary announcements after the ice-breaker activity and before getting serious. Be brief. Today you'll want to introduce the study series, and nail down the time and length of your meetings.

Introduce the group to the series by saying something like this:

**This series is designed to help us explore what the Bible says about God and our search for Him. The Bible's answers are a lot different than society's. The belief that there is a God once gave meaning to human existence. Today this assumption is no longer widely held and people are floundering in a sea of uncertainty. Is this assumption worth revisiting? If you think so, then we're going to spend the next several weeks discussing what the Bible says about filling the "God-shaped vacuum" within each of us.**

Hand out copies of the journals and explain how they can be used.

**These journals are not "homework." They are journals. They are meant to stimulate your own self-examination and self-expression. They do, however, introduce the topic that we're going to study the next week, so it's best if you set aside some time once or twice a week, at least, to do something in your journal in preparation for our time together.**

**There is a section each week called "Daily Markings" [flip to that now] where you can keep a daily diary if you want to. The idea is to jot down major events such as an important conversation, a movie you saw, something you read, or something you did that was significant; then write about how you felt about it. The idea is to look back at the end of the week as you've been doing the regular journal and see how God has been at work in your life.**

**The journal should be done before the next week's study. It can be done in one sitting in about fifteen minutes. But it might be better to spread it out over a couple of days, doing one section or so at a time.**

**One suggestion is to have group members form prayer partners who will meet at least once a week outside of the group time. These partners can share their personal thoughts with each other more deeply than they may in a group set-**

ting, and can pray for one another. If you have non-Christians in the group—and we hope you do—this can be especially important. Pair a non-Christian up with a sensitive and mature Christian so that the non-Christian can talk freely about his or her questions and doubts about Christianity. Encourage the Christians to spend time actually praying together, and not just sharing needs. Nothing bonds two Christians together to produce spiritual growth more than praying together.

Once you have decided when, where, how often, and how long you will meet, decide how you will handle leadership.

## Opening

If you have someone who can play an instrument, ask if that person would be willing to lead singing each week. You don't have to sing, of course, but there will be suggestions in this section each week of songs you could sing that go along with the theme. Most of the songs can be found in songbooks available in most Christian bookstores.

Sing a chorus such as "Seek Ye First." Then open your study by asking God to lead you and reveal Himself in whatever way is needed.

There will occasionally be suggestions in this section for creative ways to pray. Invite those who have not committed themselves to Christ, or are unsure, to listen along, but don't put them in a position where they have to lead in prayer.

# 2 Bible Study (30-45 minutes)

## Focus

For this first meeting, have group members turn to the introduction of the first unit, "Searchers One and All," on pages 8 and 9 of their journals. Give them a few minutes to read it.

### Searchers One and All

by Kelly Peavey

Every one of us is looking for love. And that's not necessarily a bad thing. We all need to feel loved, accepted, and a sense of belonging. Unfortunately, too many people look in too many wrong places to find meaning: false religions with offers too good to be true (and which aren't true), money, fame, power, status, multiple sex partners, good looks, even technology. All of these things seem to offer fulfillment, but they only leave people feeling empty and lonely.

The Bible offers the answers and points us to the love that will satisfy and fulfill us. It says that you matter to God even if you don't seem to have much significance here on earth. If you accept His offer, you can have eternal life, and that longing deep in your soul will be satisfied.

This unit will take a look at some tough questions—some eternal questions—as well as what the Bible has to say about them. And while it won't give you all of the answers, it will tell you where to start lookin' for true love.

Point out to your group that sometimes we don't want to hear the answers the Bible gives. The passage you're going to look at right now has some good news and some bad news. It's a message of judgment as well as of mercy. It's primarily a message about God and the claims He makes on those He calls His children.

Say: **In the end, it's up to you to decide if you're going to accept the answers the Bible gives or not. So, "Come now, let us reason together"** (Isaiah 1:18).

## Dig In

Explain the "rules of the game" about inductive Bible study from pages 7-10, then move into this quick study in which you will "reason together" about the basic question of God's authority to define our lives. This will not be a thorough inductive study, but will get group members used to the general technique.

Turn in your Bibles to Isaiah 1:1-20. Have someone read the entire text aloud as you all follow along.

# INSIDE INSIGHTS

■ The word "vision" in Isaiah 1:1 implies that the writer is saying he has a message from God. The author is claiming that he didn't just dream up what he's saying. The prophets of the Old Testament claimed to speak *for* God, and the people accepted their authority as the mouthpieces of the living God. The penalties against false prophets, therefore, were very severe. If just one prophecy proved false, that prophet was to be stoned (Deuteronomy 18:20-22).

■ Israel was once one nation composed of twelve tribes. After Solomon's death, the nation split in two. The northern ten tribes were called Israel; the southern two were called Judah, with Jerusalem the capital. Sometimes when the prophets in this period spoke of Israel, it was in reference to the *nation*, the ten northern tribes who broke away from the worship of the Lord. Sometimes it was in reference to the *people* and would have included Judah, which remained somewhat faithful—at least in the outward form of their religion. Isaiah seems to refer to the latter because there is a parallelism between Judah and Jerusalem in the first verse, with Israel and the phrase "my people" in the third verse.

*Observation questions:*

• Who was this written to? What kind of literature is it? What title would you give this passage?

• Who is said to be speaking from the latter part of verse 2 on? Why is this significant?

• From verse 2, what can you tell about the significance of Judah and Jerusalem to God?

• As you read over this passage, what words or phrases stand out to you about what the people are like? To whom does the Lord compare them?

*Interpretation questions:*

• Why does the Lord say He "hates" the people's religious ceremonies? What is it that He wants instead?

• What does God offer the people? What are the terms?

• Do you think this is a fair offer on God's part? Why or why not?

• Why does He say He wants to reason with them? What does this tell you about God?

• If you were to put this chapter to music, what style of music or what instruments would you use? Why?

*Application questions:*

• Are there things that bother you about this passage? If so, what?

Encourage openness here. Today, when tolerance is often considered the

highest virtue, it may be hard for some people to accept the concept of God's judgment. That's often the biggest stumbling block that keeps people from coming to Christ. But until a person acknowledges God's right to be God—to call the shots—he or she cannot really come to Christ at all. That's why, in this introductory study, we want to hit the issue straight on. Encourage people to be totally honest about their feelings concerning this kind of a God. Remember, God does not need our defense. He can speak for Himself. A person must accept or reject God on God's own terms.

• **Does anyone have a right to judge anyone else? Why or why not? What would give someone a right to judge someone else?**

• **What difference does belief in God make to a person's self-image?**

Wrap up with a summary such as this:

**For those who believe in God and accept the Bible as His revealed Word to humankind, there is both good news and bad news. The good news is that we matter to God. He loves us and wants to bless us, as Isaiah 1:18, 19 say. But there is always the condition of reciprocity. If God is God, then He has a right to lay His conditions on us. They may be for our own good, but we still resist. There are some people who cannot believe in God because they cannot live with the idea of submitting to anyone else's will. If they're right, they haven't lost anything. But if they're wrong, they will suffer the consequences of their rebellion.**

**What we're going to do in this study is take a look at the biblical foundation for our search for God.**

 # Reflect and Respond

Since you have not used your journals yet, just ask for responses to the study or to the idea of doing this series.

• **Are you willing to make the commitment to this study? Are you interested in exploring this topic from a biblical point of view and letting the Scripture speak for itself, even if you don't always like what it says?**

• **What anxieties or hopes do you have about how this study might change your life?**

If the group is ready for it, make a covenant to meet together for this study for the next fifteen weeks (or however long it will take to cover what you decide to cover). The terms of this covenant might be something like this: to be faithful

in attendance, to keep an open mind toward what the Bible has to say, to be supportive of one another and honest in sharing from the journals with at least one other person in the group.

Seal the covenant by joining hands in prayer, asking God to bless you.

# 3 Sharing and Prayer

For the rest of your time, allow people to talk about what's going on in their lives and pray for one another. You can leave this totally open-ended, or you can do something different with this time. Here's one idea:

After everyone has had a chance to share and you have spent some time in prayer, take a picture (using a Polaroid camera) of each person in the group. Have each person put his or her name and phone number on the back, along with an ongoing prayer request or concern. Collect the pictures; then distribute them as prayer cards. If you're dividing into prayer partners, this is a natural. But even if you're not, this is a good way to get people praying for each other. If you wish, you can ask people to bring the pictures back next week and trade them so that everyone will have prayed for everyone else by the time this series is over.

Remind people to do Week One in their journals for next week. Then close in prayer and go eat some goodies!

# UNIT One

# Searchers One and All

Humanity! We're always searching for something. Usually it's that thing we think will bring us security, happiness, love, or whatever we happen to be wanting at the moment.

The neighbor gets a new car, and soon we start to notice a few more rust spots on our own. "Better do something about that now, before it gets any worse." We begin to feel a little empty or lonely, and it's off to the mall. We see something we think we need, and we buy it whether we can afford it or not; we just pull out the plastic. But soon the new toy that we thought would satisfy starts to look a little dull and becomes boring, so it's off to get the next new toy to replace it.

We're a society committed to *things,* not to people, relationships, or God. We run over people as we go from one thing to another, and sometimes we get so busy that we don't even know we're running, much less that we're running over people in our way.

What are we running to—or from? What can cure the restlessness in our hearts, the emptiness that aches within? Is there really anything that can satisfy the human soul?

**About the author:** *Kelly Peavey is a former high school teacher who has worked with young people for over ten years. Married and a mother of two, Kelly is a free-lance writer. She has a degree in education from Texas Tech University and lives in Plaistow, New Hampshire, where she is active in lay ministry in her church.*

# What Is the Meaning of Life?

**Theme:** God created everyone with a purpose, and life really does have meaning.

**Scripture:** Psalm 138:8a; John 4:1-26

## 1 Getting Started

### Housekeeping

Welcome everyone to the Bible study. You may want to have people share their names and something about themselves just so everyone can get acquainted. Briefly make necessary announcements. It may be useful at this point to outline the general format and length of the Bible study so that the group members know what to expect.

### Icebreaker

Choose one of the following activities to get things rolling:

## What's the Point?

Write the following list of activities on a large piece of paper or chalkboard before the meeting. Write the heading "Possible Goals," then have members offer possible goals or purposes for each activity. As they offer their suggestions, write them down.

| Activities | Possible Goals |
|---|---|
| Running a race | To win the prize |
| Working | To earn money |
| Getting married | To have companionship |
| Going to school | To learn |

After some discussion, ask group members how they would feel about doing these activities if there was no goal. Does the goal make a difference in how they view the activities?

## Agree or Disagree?

Write the following quotes on a large piece of paper or chalkboard, or make copies for everyone in the group.

• **"The art of life is to know how to enjoy a little and to endure much."**
**—William Hazlitt**

• **"There is no cure for birth and death save to enjoy the interval."**
**—George Santayana**

• **"Nature has given man no better thing than shortness of life."**
**—Pliny the Elder**

Give everyone a piece of paper. Ask group members to select one quote and write their reasons as to why they agree or disagree with that quote. Have a few volunteers share their responses. Then ask what group members feel about the overall view presented by the quotes.

In general, these quotes show a view of the world without God. There is nothing to look forward to but the moment, and that moment is ticking away toward death. Pretty depressing!

## Opening

Sing "I Am the Resurrection" or some other song about life in and with God. Ask someone to open in prayer.

# 2 Bible Study

## Focus

Ask volunteers to share something they wrote in the "Reflection" portion of this week's journal. Ask group members to think about what motivates them, then briefly discuss the differences between living with a purpose and living without one. Which way of living would they prefer?

## Dig In

Say: **The way you view the big questions in life really makes a difference in how you live. Does life have meaning? What exactly is your purpose in life? These are biggies. There are many theories about the value of our life here on earth. The Bible says that everyone was created for a purpose and that life really does have meaning. Let's take a look.**

Have group members turn to John 4. Ask a volunteer or two to read verses 1-26.

First, ask group members questions that focus on the background of this incident.

• **Why did Jesus go through Samaria (verses 1-4)?**

See "Inside Insights" to explain the relationship between Jews and Samaritans.

• **Why was the woman surprised when Jesus asked her for a drink?**

Not only were there racial barriers between the two nationalities, there were other barriers as well. In those days, rabbis didn't speak to women other than those in their immediate family. Yet Jesus speaks openly with this woman.

- Describe Jesus' answer in verse 10 to the woman's question.

- How does He clarify His answer in verses 13 and 14?

Jesus emphasizes the fact that He offers living water. He explains that those who drink of living water will never thirst and will have eternal life.

Have a volunteer read verses 15-26. Then assess the details of this passage.

- **Why do you think Jesus asked the woman to get her husband when Jesus already knew her lifestyle?**

You are looking for opinions here. Still, encourage group members to draw their ideas from the text, rather than from their own imaginations. Jesus not only tests her to see if she will tell the truth—which she does, even though she doesn't tell everything—He also uses her answer as an opportunity to show her who He is.

- **Upon recognizing Jesus as a prophet, the woman asks Him a spiritual question regarding worship. What does this tell you about the woman?**

- **What is Jesus' answer** (verses 22-24)?

Jesus emphasizes that soon the place of worship will not be important. Rather, the condition of worship ("in spirit and in truth") will be of greatest importance. Allow for some discussion about what this type of worship would be like.

- **The woman mentions how the Messiah will explain everything when He comes. What is Jesus' answer to this statement?**

Take a look at what this incident has to say about the meaning of life and the significance of each individual. If you have a chalkboard handy, you may want to list group members' responses.

- **What characteristics of the Samaritan woman might have prevented Jesus from speaking to her?**

She was a Samaritan woman with a wild lifestyle.

- **Yet how does Jesus respond to her? Does He accept or reject her? Explain.**

Jesus speaks to her respectfully. He answers her questions, though sometimes not directly, in a way that allows her to see some important truths.

- **What is Jesus' purpose in talking with this woman?**

This is about more than a drink of water. Jesus talks with her about living water that satisfies completely and leads to eternal life. He shares with her how to truly worship. And He tells her directly that He is the Messiah. This is the only recorded time He openly admitted this until the great confession (in Matthew 16). Just looking at these facts leads to the conclusion that the woman's life mattered to Him. He cared.

• **How does Jesus' response to this woman relate to how God values each individual and the meaning of each person's life today?**

As God in the flesh, Jesus responded as God the Father would respond. Jesus cared enough about the Samaritan woman to reveal truths about Himself and God the Father. These truths had the power to change her life forever. If God cared about her, then He must care about us too. And if Jesus went to such trouble to help this "unacceptable" woman find meaning in life, there really must be meaning and purpose in life after all.

 ## Reflect and Respond

Close with a couple of questions for personal application and reflection.

• **What do you think the Samaritan woman looked to in order to find meaning? Why was she so interested in the "living water" Jesus talked about? Do you think her life was satisfying her? Explain.**

# INSIDE INSIGHTS

■ The Jewish nation split after the death of King Solomon. The northern tribes made Samaria their capital city. Later, Assyria attacked and destroyed the capital, and conquered and resettled the land with other conquered people. This mixed population practiced mixed religion, combining pagan and Jewish faiths. This practice caused the Jews to despise the Samaritans even more than other Gentiles because they felt the Samaritans were worshiping God in a corrupt way. In turn, the Samaritans despised the Jews for rejecting them. Often the Jews would go out of their way to avoid Samaria, and the Samaritans would refuse hospitality to Jewish travelers.

• How do you think Jesus would respond to the question "Does life have meaning?"

Allow time for group members to share thoughts from the study or from their journals. You may want to ask how God's value of life affects their views of the meaning of life and their particular purposes in life.

### Leadership Tip

Don't be afraid of a few moments of silence. Sometimes it takes a quiet moment for people to formulate their thoughts before they share. The silence may seem like an eternity to you, but it won't seem that way to the rest of the group. If it's a struggle to allow some quiet moments, try counting to fifteen before moving on to the next question or statement.

# 3 Sharing and Prayer

Allow group members to briefly share personal concerns and prayer requests; then spend at least ten minutes in prayer. You may pray together as a group or break into smaller groups.

Close the meeting by reading Psalm 138:8a as a benediction, emphasizing God's purpose and love for all—"The Lord will fulfill his purpose for me; your love, O Lord, endures forever."

# Looking for God among the Gods

**Theme:** There is only one true God.

**Scripture:** I Chronicles 16:26; Psalm 34:4-8; Romans 1:18-25

# 1 Getting Started

## Housekeeping

Greet group members, welcome newcomers, and make any necessary introductions and announcements.

## Icebreaker

Choose one of the following activities to begin the meeting:

### God Defined

Have group members divide into groups of three to five. Give each group a piece of poster board or a large piece of paper and some markers. Explain that their task is to write a definition of God—who He is, what He is like, what He does, etc. For those who don't believe in God, have them write what they would like God to be if He did exist.

After a few minutes, have groups share what they've come up with. Don't criticize any viewpoint. Remember, group members are opening up a part of themselves in this activity, and everyone should be respected. After all groups have shared, display the posters in the room to use later in the study if you'd like.

## Your Choice

Read the following scenario and have group members decide if they would choose Response A or Response B.

**A loving and wise benefactor desires to give you twenty billion dollars. On which terms would you prefer to receive the money?**

> **A. You must spend the money wisely, always be kind and do good, visit your benefactor at least once a week, do a good deed every day, and spend a few moments a day being thankful for your gift and your benefactor.**

> **B. You must accept the gift completely without reservation, allow the generosity of the gift to change your life completely—the way you think, act, eat, sleep, and live—and seek to do what your benefactor would want you to do.**

You may need to point out the differences between the two choices. One requires a person to be kind and good, and to do good things; the other requires the person to change completely to live as the benefactor wishes. After a few minutes, have group members offer their responses. Jot answers down on the board (if you have one) to use later in the study.

## Leadership Tip

Use the information and ideas shared during the "Icebreaker" to draw group members into the Bible study in a personal way. For example, you can use their definitions of God or the choices they made in the second icebreaker activity as a reference when you discuss the advantages and disadvantages of inventing your own god. Members can use their previous comments as a springboard for offering more in-depth ideas. Also, those who are quiet may feel more comfortable if they have something to refer to when they speak.

## Opening

Have someone read I Chronicles 16:26. Open with prayer, asking God to distinguish Himself among other "gods" through the study of His Word. Thank Him for being willing to show Himself to us.

# 2 Bible Study

### Focus

Have group members turn to this week's introduction in their journals. Ask some volunteers to respond to the questions "Is God something humans made up to calm our fears and make sense of the world? Or is God really God?"

After a few people share, follow up with these questions:

• **What are some advantages of inventing your own god?**

• **What are some disadvantages?**

Though creating our own gods may give us the opportunity to make a god that approves of our every whim, that doesn't amount to a hill of beans if our god isn't real. And if we worship our own creation instead of the true God, we really have no resource but ourselves.

### Dig In

Read Romans 1:18-25 to the group. Ask group members to share what stands out from what they've just heard. Responses may include God's anger, punishment for sin, humans' creation of gods, and the consequences that follow.

Group members may be surprised at the Bible's blunt account of what happens when we seek after other gods. Many people like to see only the benevolent side of God. It's not easy to consider the wrath of God and the consequences for our actions, but burying our heads in the sand doesn't get us any closer to the truth. It is better to see the cliff and move cautiously, than to race off the cliff blindly to certain doom.

Have a volunteer read Romans 1:18-20. Then follow up with these questions:

• **What do these verses say about humans and their knowledge of God?**

• **Verse 18 talks about people who "suppress the truth." What does that mean? How might a person "suppress the truth"?**

• **According to verse 20, what should all people know about God?**

Have a volunteer read verses 21-23. Then follow up with these questions:

• **How did people respond to God?**

• **What was the result?**

Verse 21 points to darkened, futile thinking. Verse 22 mentions people becoming fools while thinking themselves wise. Verse 23 addresses people exchanging God's glory for images of other people, birds, animals, and reptiles.

Have a volunteer read verses 24 and 25. Then follow up with these questions:

• **What did God allow to occur?**

• **Notice the phrase, "Because of this, God gave them over to shameful lusts." Who really caused this to occur? Explain.**

• **This passage asserts that people knew of God before they made their decisions to "suppress the truth." They made their choice and must face the consequences. Can you apply this passage to today? If so, in what way?**

• **Often we talk of God being loving and merciful. Why do you think God's wrath is revealed in this situation?**

God is a God of love, but He refuses to make our choices for us. He doesn't want a bunch of Christian robots. People are responsible for their choices and the consequences that follow. God is merciful, but He will not force someone to choose what is right.

• **This passage shows the negative results of rejecting God for our own desires. What do you think are the positive results of accepting God and His ways?**

## Reflect and Respond

Read Psalm 34:4-8 to the group. Have group members bow their heads and pray silently as you guide them with the following words. Leave a few seconds between each thought for group members to reflect.

Lord, we have seen today what can happen when we invent our own gods. . . . Help us know the truth and not suppress it. . . . Show us now things that we are putting before You. . . . Give us wisdom to seek the true God. . . . Please take away anything that may keep us from the truth. . . . In Jesus' name. Amen.

# 3 Sharing and Prayer

Allow a few minutes for requests and praises. Encourage group members to pray for society and the idols we have created. Be sure to actually pray at least ten minutes. If some of your group members are shy about praying out loud, reassure them that you will not force anyone to pray aloud and that God hears our silent prayers as well as our verbal ones.

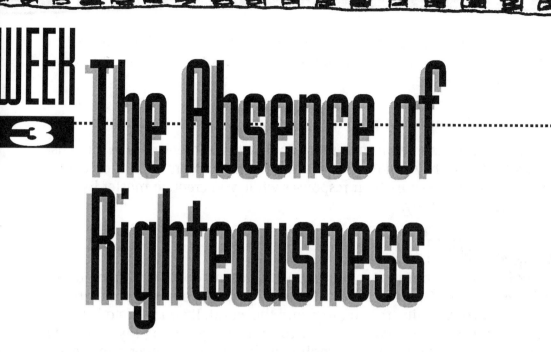

# WEEK 3
# The Absence of Righteousness

**Theme:** Without God there is no righteousness.

**Scripture:** Psalm 14; I Corinthians 15:32

# 1 Getting Started

### Housekeeping

Welcome group members and make necessary announcements. If there are newcomers, you may wish to make them more comfortable by briefly sharing what the group has studied over the past two sessions.

### Icebreaker

Choose one of the following activities to begin the meeting:

**No Rules**

Have group members divide into groups of two or three. Give each group a

large sheet of paper and markers. Allow three minutes for each group to draw a picture of a society with no rules, laws, or values. Allow each group to talk briefly about its picture.

**What's Really Wrong with the World Today Is . . .**

Give group members a few minutes to complete this sentence. Have them list as many things as they can think of while working in pairs or on their own. Then allow people to share their responses while you create a master list to refer to later in the study.

## Opening

It's not hard to see that many things are going wrong in our world today. Open the study in prayer, guiding your group members to pray for your community, the country, and the world. If you made a list of "what's wrong with the world today," encourage the group to pray specifically for things mentioned on that list. Emphasize the power of prayer and the fact that through prayer, we can make a difference.

### Leadership Tip

Praying aloud can be difficult, especially for those who haven't done it before. Here are some ways to encourage participation without putting people on the spot.

• Have group members pray single-sentence prayers. This relieves the pressure of feeling like they have to say a lot.

• Guide the prayer topically by making an introduction for each topic, then allowing people to respond. For example, if you opened the prayer with, "Lord, hear us as we offer our praise to You," then group members would follow by offering words of praise. Throughout the prayer you can introduce topics for group members to follow, such as thanksgiving, requests, etc.

• Pray one-word prayers. It may be easier to do this when you are praying topically. For example, if praying for the needs of the community, one-word prayers might include "peace," "safety," "hope," etc.

# ❷ Bible Study

## Focus

• The apostle Paul says in I Corinthians 15:32, "If the dead are not raised, 'Let us eat and drink, for tomorrow we die.' " What do you think he means by that?

While emphasizing the importance of Christ's resurrection and the future resurrection of believers, Paul points out that without the hope of eternal life, our earthly lives don't mean much. People "eat and drink," or seek earthly pleasures, then die.

• Is pleasure what motivates people today? Is that what motivates you?

• How does this focus on pleasure affect our society?

Refer group members to the quotes in the introduction of this week's journal session. Ask your group members why they think there is so much evil in the world if people are actually seeking pleasure. You may also wish to allow time for them to share their journal responses to this question.

## Dig In

Read Psalm 14 as a group by having each member read one verse until the psalm is completed. It's a short passage, so not everyone may get a turn to read.

• How is the fool described in verse 1? What are his distinguishing characteristics?

• In verse 2, what does God do? Why do you think He does this?

There may be some speculation as to the details, but one thing is clear: God cares about the conduct of people and He desires for them to seek Him.

• What is being described in verse 3?

Notice that "they have together become corrupt." This is not a few bad choices, but a deliberate lifestyle chosen by the people.

Have someone read Psalm 14:4-7. Then ask the following questions:

• **How does the psalmist describe evildoers?**

Focus the group's attention on the image in verse 4, "as men eat bread." This daily, ordinary occurrence is used to describe the ruthlessness of evildoers.

• **Where is God when all of this evil is taking place?**

Verse 5 shows Him "in the company of the righteous." Verse 6 shows Him as a refuge for the poor.

• **How do the wicked react?**

• **Where does the psalmist look for deliverance from this evil?**

• **In what way do the descriptions of the evildoer apply to today's society?**

• **In verse 4, the psalmist asks, "Will evildoers never learn?" After reading newspaper headlines or watching the evening news, how would you answer this question? What differences do you see between our society and the one described by the psalmist?**

## Reflect and Respond

Say: **Psalm 14:2 says, "The Lord looks down from heaven on the sons of men to see if there are any who understand, any who seek God." What do you think God sees as He looks down on earth today?**

After some discussion on God's view of society, bring the application a little closer to home. Ask group members what they think God sees when He looks down at each one of them. Hand out sheets of paper and pencils and have group members respond to Psalm 14:2 with words or a picture. You may want to reread the verse aloud as they begin or encourage them to work with their Bibles open.

After about five minutes, allow discussion time for those who would like to share. Don't pressure anyone to talk, just let the conversation flow naturally. This is pretty personal stuff! Encourage group members to take home what they've written or drawn, and reflect on it in the coming week.

# 3 Sharing and Prayer

Encourage group members to share concerns and prayer requests. If they prefer to pray in smaller groups, allow time for them to move into their groups. Allow a few minutes for prayer, encouraging group members to pray for the requests and concerns that were shared earlier.

# INSIDE INSIGHTS

■ *Fool*—The word fool (*nabal*) doesn't necessarily mean an atheist, but rather a person who lives as if God didn't exist.

*Salvation*—In the Old Testament, salvation relates both to earthly needs and the life to come in heaven. It can refer to deliverance from the difficulties of life, such as illness, persecution, war, and death. It also refers to messianic salvation when God Himself would come to save His people.

*Zion*—In the Old Testament, Zion is used as another name for the temple, the Jewish meeting place with God. It is the name for the religious center for the Jewish people.

# WEEK 4: It's Not Fair!

**Theme:** Life doesn't always seem fair, but in the end people reap what they sow.

**Scripture:** Matthew 5:45b; 19:28-30; Luke 6:17-26; Galatians 6:7-9

# 1 Getting Started

## Housekeeping

Welcome group members, and make necessary introductions and announcements. You may also wish to bring in refreshments for the group to share at this time.

## Icebreaker

Choose one of the following activities to begin the meeting:

**Yankee Swap (Modified)**

Before group members arrive, wrap some small gifts in tissue paper. Gifts might include a piece of bubble gum, a lollipop, a cookie, a pencil, etc. Also wrap a few rocks. As people arrive, give each of them a "gift" and ask them to wait to open them. Make sure that you give away a few rocks. After announcements, allow group members to open their gifts one at a time. Before opening the gift, however, the person has the option of trading it with any opened gift in the room. After all gifts are opened, talk briefly about how it felt to receive each gift, how it felt to receive a rock, and how it felt to have something "good" exchanged for a rock. Was the gift exchange "fair"?

## Who Benefits?

Read the following scenarios to the group. After reading each one, have group members respond to the following questions.

*Scenario 1*

You are taking a big test in geometry that you've studied for all week. You need to make at least a B to pass the class. The person behind you keeps tapping you on the shoulder and asking you for answers. Finally, in frustration, you turn around to tell him to leave you alone. Your teacher accuses both of you of cheating and gives you both a zero on the test.

*Scenario 2*

You go into a convenience store for some gum and a soda. You give the cashier a ten-dollar bill. You take the change and go out to your car. Once inside your car, you notice that he gave you change for a twenty.

- **How do you feel?**
- **Is this fair?**
- **What are the repercussions of this?**
- **What can be done to make things right?**

Wrap up this activity by asking if the cases are similar or different from each other. Ask volunteers to explain their answers.

 ## Opening

Have group members close their eyes and concentrate while you read Matthew 19:28-30. Then open the session in prayer, asking God to reveal His truth through His word.

# 2 Bible Study

## Focus

Refer group members to their journals. Read Matthew 5:45b aloud, and ask volunteers to share their thoughts and reactions to the verse.

Then ask: **What does Jesus mean when He says, "But many who are first will be last, and many who are last will be first"** (Matthew 19:30)? **Does this verse contradict Matthew 5:45? Explain.**

Matthew 19:30 may seem like a riddle for some in the group, so you may need to guide them by asking who might be considered "first" in our world today. Who is "last"? Help group members recognize that Jesus is talking about spiritual values versus material values. While God may not withhold earthly or material wealth from the wicked, the conclusion of the matter is that spiritual values are eternal and material values are temporary. No matter how much you possess here on earth, if you don't know Christ and have eternal life, it's all going to seem worthless in the end.

### Leadership Tip

By this point in your discussion, some of your group members—especially those who are not Christians—may be wondering about the many wealthy Christians in our society. If so, this would be a good time to discuss the fact that it's not the material possessions themselves that are bad, but rather our attitude toward those possessions that can become sinful.

## Dig In

Have someone read Luke 6:17-19. Then ask these questions to set the scene.

- Describe the people who came to see Jesus and why they had come.

- How would you describe the atmosphere (verse 19)?

Read in unison verses 20-26. You may want to copy this passage and hand it out to group members before you start so that everyone is reading from the same translation.

Jesus is talking to His disciples about their lifestyle and the choices they will make in their lives as they follow Him. His words tell us a lot about the rewards for our choices and actions.

Write group members' responses to the next two questions on a chalkboard or a large sheet of paper. As a group, diagram what Jesus says and then use this for further analysis.

**• Why are the following called blessed: the poor; those who hunger; those who weep; those who are rejected, insulted, and hated for Jesus' sake?**

Those people are blessed because they will receive an eternal reward. The poor will inherit the kingdom of God. Those who hunger will be satisfied. Those who weep will laugh. Those who are rejected, insulted, and hated for Jesus' sake will be rewarded as the prophets were.

**• Why does Jesus say "woe" to the following people: those who are rich, those who are well fed, those who laugh, and those who are well spoken of?**

These are people who have chosen to go after earthly pleasures. Those who are rich have already received comfort. Those who are well fed will go hungry. Those who laugh will mourn and weep. Those who are well spoken of will be treated as the false prophets were.

Look back at what you have diagrammed and do some reading between the lines. Jesus describes people who are outwardly considered unfortunate; yet Jesus calls them blessed. Take a closer look as these people using the following questions:

**• Who are the poor?**

The financially poor, the poor in spirit, and the poor in circumstances.

**• Who are the hungry?**

Those who are hungry for food and those who are hungry for righteousness.

**• Who are those who weep?**

Those who are lonely, sorrowful, and brokenhearted.

• Why would people hate, insult, and exclude someone because of the person's faith in Jesus?

• Describe the value of the rewards for these people.

No money could ever buy the kingdom of God, eternal life, or great rewards in heaven.

• What is the value of wealth, food, happiness, and people's approval? How long-lasting is it?

• What do you imagine those who "laugh now" are laughing about? How long will their laughter last?

The pleasures of life are temporary. They come and go, and are not dependable. But the things of the Spirit last forever.

 ## Reflect and Respond

Say: **Even though at times it looks like the bad guys are getting ahead by leaps and bounds, God's Word says that in the end everyone will get what he or she deserves.**

Read Galatians 6:7, 8. Have group members reflect a moment on the direction of their lives. Then pray that the Spirit of God would guide each person to choose eternal life. Close by reading Galatians 6:9 as a benediction.

■ *Blessed*—The word *makarios* is used in reference to people, meaning a state of happiness. It also relates a strong spiritual sense as Jesus uses it to describe humans. People who are called "blessed" often appear outwardly to deserve pity for the condition of their lives; yet inside their spiritual condition is honorable.

*Woe*—This Greek interjection (*ovai*) means "alas for." Jesus uses it to describe the wretched, miserable state of people who neglect or ignore their spiritual selves. Often they are motivated by wealth, popularity, fame, and self-satisfaction and lack compassion, love, and the desire for truth.

# 3 Sharing and Prayer

Allow time for group members to share prayer requests, but also spend some of your prayer time praying for justice in the world. Close by asking for wisdom and strength for each of your group members to choose the right way.

# Can't Get No Satisfaction

**Theme:** Only God can offer true satisfaction.

**Scripture:** Psalm 145:13b-16; Isaiah 55

## 1 Getting Started

### Housekeeping

Welcome any newcomers to the group and make sure that they are introduced to everyone else at the meeting. Then make any necessary announcements.

### Icebreaker

Choose one of the following activities to begin the meeting:

**Then I Would Be Happy**

Have group members complete this sentence: "If I just had _____ , then I would be happy." After a minute or two, ask volunteers to share their answers.

Write their responses on the left side of a chalkboard or large sheet of paper. Then go back and have group members define the expectations for each response. For example, for "popularity," the expectation is lots of friends, acceptance, fun, boyfriends or girlfriends, etc. Afterward, ask whether these things really bring fulfillment.

### Following Directions

Create a short treasure hunt with about five clues. Have group members divide into two teams. Give each team the first clue in an envelope. Teams should open the clue at the same time. This clue should lead to the second clue, and so on until the treasure is found. The team that gets to the treasure first wins. The treasure can be anything you like—Scripture bookmarks, bubble gum, you name it.

After the hunt, ask group members how they felt about the clues, competition, and prizes. Were they satisfied with the outcome of the hunt? Why or why not?

## Opening

Have someone read Psalm 145:13b-16. Then sing a song like "Jehovah-Jireh" about God's provision for our needs. Open in prayer, thanking God for His fulfillment of our needs as shown in Psalm 145.

# 2 Bible Study

## Focus

Say: The Rolling Stones' song "(I Can't Get No) Satisfaction" is the unofficial theme song of many people today. Though they try and try, they just can't find the fulfillment they are looking for.

Ask group members where they see people looking for satisfaction today. As group members share their responses, make a list of the things people try as they're seeking satisfaction and fulfillment (money, new religions, fame, etc.). Then encourage group members to share from the "Response" section

of their journal this week regarding where they are looking for satisfaction. Has their search left them satisfied or dissatisfied?

 ## Dig In

Read Isaiah 55:1, 2 aloud. Then ask the following questions:

• **Who is the invitation in this passage issued to? What are these people invited to do?**

• **What is Isaiah talking about in verse 2?**

Allow group members to speculate on what "is not bread" and "does not satisfy." Listing some of their ideas may help them apply what they are discovering to their own lives.

### Leadership Tip

It's much easier to look at "all of those other people out there" and point out their faults than it is to see our own. It is an even harder thing to admit our faults to someone else. You may want to give your group members paper, pencils, and some quiet time to reflect and write down some of what they're seeing in themselves.

Have someone read Isaiah 55:3-5. Then ask the following questions:

• **What is the result of listening to what the Lord has to say** (verse 3)?

• **What has God done through David** (verses 4 and 5)?

Through the line of David—through his offspring (Jesus)—God has reached the world.

Read verses 6 and 7 aloud. Then ask the following questions:

• **What should be our reaction to God, according to these verses?**

• **What is the result of these actions** (verse 7)?

God is ready and willing to forgive if we only will turn to Him.

Read verses 8-13 as a group, having each member read one verse until the passage is completed.

• **How is God described in verses 8-11?**

■ The overall theme of Isaiah 55 is turning unreservedly to God in faith for life, which means a change of behavior.

Commands to buy without money show that true grace equals total dependence on God's gifts without any merit of our own.

David, in verse 3, refers to the promises to King David of the Messiah as the text points to God's deliverance of Israel.

The rain and snow images in verse 10 convey the sense of an inconspicuous work that slowly transforms the face of the earth.

His thoughts are not like people's thoughts. His ways are not like people's ways. His ways are higher than people's ways. His thoughts are higher than people's thoughts. His Word will accomplish His desires and purpose.

• **Notice the images used to describe God's ways. How does that clarify what God is like?**

By taking aspects of nature that people are familiar with, God shows us how His ways are more complete and superior to ours. Images not only enable us to understand, but also paint a picture in our minds for us to hold on to in remembering who God is.

• **How does God satisfy (verse 12)?**

• **In verse 2, the Lord says "your soul will delight in the richest of fare." What do you think would delight your soul?**

• **Do people today seek to satisfy their souls, or are they out to satisfy something else? Explain.**

• **Take a look at verse 12. How do joy and peace figure into satisfaction?**

• **How do human efforts to satisfy compare with God's? Are there any surprises for you about the way God works? If so, explain.**

## Reflect and Respond

Hand out pieces of paper and pencils. Have group members draw their own personal "stores" of satisfaction. Have them draw out floor plans and fill their stores with things they've looked to for satisfaction. You may want to draw a sample for the group so that they get the idea. After a few minutes, allow for some sharing. What have members tried (or done) to find satisfaction throughout their lives? What are they looking to now? How does God fit into all of this? Close by reading Isaiah 55:6, 7 while group members join hands.

# 3 Sharing and Prayer

Ask for any prayer concerns or praises from the group. Encourage group members to pray about their own searches for satisfaction and that each one in the group may find the true Source of satisfaction for his or her life.

# UNIT Two

# What I'm Searching For

Have you ever stood in front of your closet yelling, "I can't find my blue sweater"? You've searched high and low and are convinced that aliens have come and taken it away. Then your roommate, sister, mother—anyone within hearing range who is tired of your yelling—walks up and says, "You mean this blue sweater?" and proceeds to pull it off the shelf directly in front of you.

How do we become so blind to that which is so clear, so obvious?

Each of us is born with a longing for home, a longing for purpose, a longing for meaning. Throughout the ages people have looked to many things to fulfill that longing, from various religions to fame and fortune, and even to ourselves. We have found varying degrees of success in those searchings, for a time anyway. Ultimately, anything here on earth that humans have tried to use to fill their souls has failed.

There is only one thing that can truly fulfill and satisfy our souls. In this unit, we will discover, indeed, what we are searching for.

*About the author:* *Laurel Edison works in Washington, D.C. She is fluent in German, having studied at Tübingen University in Germany. She graduated from the University of Michigan, where as part of her program she taught creative writing in prisons.*

# WEEK 6

# Whence This Longing?

**Theme:** People are born with a longing that can be completely satisfied only by God.

**Scripture:** Acts 17

# 1 Getting Started

## Housekeeping

Make any necessary announcements regarding meeting time and location. If you have any newcomers, be sure to make introductions and to make them feel welcome.

## Icebreaker

Buy several bags of M&Ms. Distribute five M&Ms to each person, making sure that everyone receives every color (yellow, brown, red, orange, green). Explain that the colors represent the following categories: yellow = family; brown = hobbies/interests; red = dreams/aspirations; orange = something unusual about yourself; green = work/school.

Let group members eat their M&Ms, but explain first that as they eat each one, they must share a longing they have in the area of life that color represents. This exercise can vary in length; you may opt to cover all five categories or you may limit the selection to as few as two categories. You also may need to vary the instructions depending on the willingness of your group members to share.

## Opening

Give each group member a piece of paper and a pencil. Ask each person to jot down anything that is currently cluttering his or her mind. Spend several minutes in silent prayer, quieting yourselves before God and giving your plans and worries to Him. Have someone pray aloud to conclude this time of prayer.

# 2 Bible Study

### Leadership Tip

If you have quiet people in your group, this doesn't mean that they have nothing to say. Perhaps they need some time to "warm up" and feel comfortable. Try asking them if they have anything to add, but don't push them. Include them by asking them to read. Never minimalize what anyone has to say.

## Focus

Ask: **What do modern people seek? Where are they looking?**

As group members offer suggestions, write them on a large piece of paper or chalkboard. When group members have exhausted their ideas, look at the list and identify any common categories or themes that have emerged. Talk briefly about the things people seek and the longings and needs we all have (such as love, belonging, safety, etc.).

Ask: **Are people finding what they're looking for? Give examples.**

Whether your group members have just begun their searches or long ago found the answers, they will all know people who are at various places in their journeys. Encourage group members to think of others they know, and without naming names, share some of their journeys.

## Dig In

Read Acts 17. Then ask the following study questions, which focus on Acts 17:16-28.

• Luke, a physician and one of Paul's traveling companions, wrote the Book of Acts (see Luke 1:1-4 and Acts 1:1, 2). Who were Paul and Luke waiting for in Acts 17:16?

• Paul noticed that the city of Athens was full of idols. How did he respond?

• Paul had two different types of audiences. Describe each of them.

• How did the Epicurean [pronounced epp-ih-kyu-REE-uhn] and Stoic philosophers respond to Paul's message in verses 18-21?

• What can you learn about the Areopagus [pronounced air-ee-AHP-uh-guss] from looking at verses 19-22?

• Describe the Athenians, based on verses 21-23.

• Why does Paul refer to the altar to the "unknown god" in verse 23?

• In verses 24-26, Paul reveals the identity of the unknown god. According to Paul, what are God's attributes? How does this God differ from the idols of Athens?

• According to Paul, what is God's relationship to humans?

• In verse 27, Paul states, "God did this so that men would seek him." What did God do and why would it make people seek Him?

• What does Paul mean when he states that God is "not far from each one of us" (see verses 27 and 28)?

## Reflect and Respond

Have your group members reflect on the implications of the following statement: "We are God's offspring."

Ask: **How do you think people would respond if Paul were to preach the same message today?** Encourage several group members to respond.

# INSIDE INSIGHTS

■ In ancient times, Athens had a population of at least a quarter of a million people. It was the seat of Greek art, science, and philosophy, and was the most important university city in the ancient world—even under Roman sway.

■ Epicurean philosophers followed the teachings of Epicurus, who lived from 341-270 B.C. Epicurus taught that nature, rather than reason, is true reality. He held that only atoms (matter) and void truly exist. Epicurus believed that humans' purpose was to achieve happiness by living a life of pleasure and avoiding pain.

Stoic philosophers believed that the true essence of humans is the mind (i.e., the capacity to understand the rational order). Stoics assented to a determinism which made all events necessary and thus reduced evil to a mere appearance. This determinism enabled them to cultivate a detachment from the world and allowed them to gain mastery over their reactions. Stoicism was austere; it excluded pity, pardon, and the expression of genuine feeling.

■ The Areopagus was a council that met on Mars Hill (a rocky hill jutting out from the western side of the Acropolis). In New Testament times, this council was charged with questions regarding morals and the rights of teachers who lectured in public.

Then say: **Explain the human heart's tendency toward worship.**

# 3 Sharing and Prayer

Have group members share prayer requests. Then give them some time to pray together. When someone makes a request, ask for a volunteer who will remember to pray for that specific request during the week ahead.

# WEEK 7 — What's the Problem?

**Theme:** The sinful nature of humans creates a separation from God.

**Scripture:** Romans 3:9-23

# 1 Getting Started

## Housekeeping

After making your necessary announcements, allow a brief time for group members to make any announcements they have regarding the group.

## Icebreaker

### The Great Divide

Prior to your meeting, cover one wall of your meeting area with large sheets of paper. Draw a large diagonal gash across the paper to represent sin. As group members arrive, have them draw or write on one side of the gash what they think life would be like if there were no sin—in other words, what life will be like when we are in the presence of God. On the other side of the gash, encourage them to draw or write a description of life separated from God. After a few minutes, allow time for discussion of what has been drawn.

## Opening

Sing one or two songs focusing on God's majestic, holy nature. Some possibilities might include "Crown Him With Many Crowns," "Holy, Holy, Holy," and "Majesty."

# 2 Bible Study

### Leadership Tip

Make an effort to involve different people in the leading of your group. Ask if someone would be willing to plan and organize a social or service event. Ask if someone else would be willing to call participants weekly to remind them of the study. Put another person in charge of organizing snacks. In addition, you should be rotating Bible study leadership responsibilities.

## Focus

Ask several in the group to share their descriptions of a sinner from the "Reflection" section of their journals. As group members share their thoughts, make a list of the characteristics described, or draw a caricature of a person having those qualities. Then prompt discussion on whether or not a person must look like the character described in order to be a sinner. Why or why not?

## Dig In

Read Romans 3:9. Then ask the following question:

• **The apostle Paul wrote the Book of Romans. To whom, then, does the pronoun "we" refer? Look at the preceding verses.**

Paul states that both Jews and Gentiles are "under sin."

Read Romans 3:10-18. Then ask the following questions:

• According to these verses—which are taken from the Old Testament—what characterizes those who are "under sin"?

• "There is no one righteous . . . there is . . . no one who seeks God . . . there is no one who does good, not even one" (Romans 3:10-12). What is your reaction to these all-inclusive statements? What does it mean to be righteous? What does it mean to be good? What does it mean to seek God?

• It seems relatively easy to call deceit, cursing, bitterness, and the shedding of blood evil. Yet verse 18 seems to sum up these evils in the statement, "There is no fear of God before their eyes." What is the fear of God? Why is it important?

Read Romans 3:19, 20. Then ask the following questions:

• What is the purpose of the law?

• What is the law? Would we be conscious of sin if it did not exist?

Read Romans 3:21-23. Then ask the following questions:

• Describe the new righteousness.

• How do we acquire this righteousness? Why do we need it?

• According to Romans 3:23, what is sin?

 ## Reflect and Respond

Ask: **Why is sin a problem?** Encourage several group members to respond.

Then ask: **Is righteousness a state of being or a type of activity? Explain.**

God says that righteousness is a gift received through faith. Reflect on the concept of righteousness as a gift.

INSIDE
INSIGHTS

■ There are three parts in the arrangement of the books of the Hebrew Old Testament—the Law, the Prophets, and the Writings. The Law is made up of the first five books of the Old Testament (also known as the Pentateuch). The Prophets can be divided into two categories: the former and the latter. The former prophets include the books of Joshua, Judges, I and II Samuel, and I and II Kings. The latter prophets are Isaiah, Jeremiah, Ezekiel, and the "Twelve."

# 3 Sharing and Prayer

Have several people share the collages they created in the "Reaction" section of their journals.

After this time of sharing, spend several minutes in silent confession. End your time of prayer by offering up praise to God for His gift of righteousness.

# WEEK 8 God Reaches Out

**Theme:** God wasn't willing to leave us in our sin, separated from Him.

**Scripture:** Matthew 27:27-31; Ephesians 2:1-10; 3:14-21; Philippians 1:3-11; Colossians 1:3-14

# 1 Getting Started

## Housekeeping

Announce any upcoming social events. If you've appointed someone to coordinate social activities, let him or her make the announcement. Remind group members to bring their wallets for next week's icebreaker.

## Icebreaker

Write words or phrases from Matthew 27:27-31 on slips of paper, making sure that you have enough slips for everyone in your group. (If you have a larger group, you may need to use additional verses from the Scripture passages listed above.) When group members arrive, hand out the slips in a random order. When everyone has arrived, have group members line up in "gym order" (shortest to tallest) and read their slips in that order. Obviously the passage will make no sense. Then allow a few minutes for them to organize themselves in the correct order, and read the passage again. Talk briefly about what confusion resulted when the words of this Scripture passage weren't in the correct order, when words that were supposed to be together were separated from each other. Explain that separation from God results in confusion in our lives, but fortunately, He provided a way out of that confusion.

## Opening

Ask one person to read "The revolutionary" by Luci Shaw and another person to read Matthew 27:27-31, in that order. The others may want to close their eyes while they listen.

**The revolutionary**
Do you
wince when you hear his name
made vanity?

What if you were not so safe
sheltered, circled by love
and convention?
What if .
the world shouted at you?
Could you take the string
of hoarse words—glutton,
wino, devil, crazy
man, agitator, bastard,
nigger-lover, rebel,
and hang the grimy ornament
around your neck
and answer
love?

See the sharp stones poised
against your head! even
your dear friend
couples your name with curses
("By God! I know not God!")
the obscene affirmation
of infidelity
echoes, insistent,
from a henhouse roof.

Then—Slap! Spit! the whip,
the thorn. The gravel
grinds your fallen knees
under a whole world's weight
until
the hammering home of all
your innocence
stakes you, stranded,
halfway between hilltop and heaven
(neither will have you).
And will you whisper
forgive?

# 2 Bible Study

*Leadership Tip*

While discussing the Bible, encourage group members to stick to the text. Challenge them to use words or verses from within the passage to support their conclusions. This allows everyone to contribute meaningfully and prevents people with extensive knowledge of the Bible from intimidating those for whom the Scriptures may be new. Occasionally it will be appropriate to cite other passages, but try to make this the exception, rather than the rule.

## Focus

Ask group members to recall times when they have seen a dead person or animal. If someone is willing, have him or her describe the experience. What are the characteristics of death?

Then ask: **Why is death intimidating for so many people, and often very difficult to talk about? Or is it?**

Ask group members to think about violent movies and TV shows they've seen, and discuss briefly how the programs have impacted society's sensitivity to death. Then imagine together how you would respond if someone who had died came back to life.

## Dig In

Ask someone to read Ephesians 2:1-10 aloud. Then ask the following questions:

• To whom and by whom is this passage written?

• Who is Paul describing in verses 1-3? What words does he use to characterize these individuals?

• Verses 1 and 2 read, "You were dead in your transgressions and sins, in which you used to live." How can you be dead in something and live in it at the same time? What kind of death is Paul referring to?

• What are the "ways of this world" (verse 2)?

• What can we learn about the "ruler of the kingdom of the air" (verse 2) by looking at the text?

• In verse 3, Paul states, "We were by nature objects of wrath." Whose wrath was directed toward us?

• According to verses 4-8, what was God's response to our dead, disobedient, sinful state? Why did He respond this way?

• What is grace? How are we saved through it?

• What does it mean to be "in Christ Jesus" (verses 6 and 7)?

• In verse 9, Paul talks about "works." What does he mean by works, and what do they have to do with our salvation?

• If, as God's workmanship, we were created to do good works, what happens when we do not do these good works?

## Reflect and Respond

Say: Ephesians 2:8 explains that salvation through faith is "the gift of God." Have you received and opened this gift? Or are you still dead in your sins?

Do you believe that you are God's workmanship? How might believing this alter your view of yourself?

As you interact with others, remember that they, too, are God's workmanship. How might this influence the way you treat them?

# 3 Sharing and Prayer

 Let volunteers share their poems, allegories, or lists of questions from the "Reaction" section of their journals.

Have group members pray for each other using Scripture as a model. Allow them to choose their own passage or use one of these: Philippians 1:3-11; Ephesians 3:14-21; Colossians 1:3-14.

■ According to the *Eerdman's Pulpit Commentary*, the reference to "air" in Ephesians 2:2 seems to suggest "that evil spirits who tempt us have their abode in the atmosphere or haunt it—like it, invisible, yet exercising an influence over human souls."

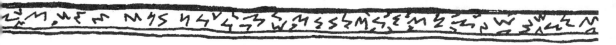

# How Will You Answer?

**Theme:** God offers a gift of salvation; it's up to us to accept it.

**Scripture:** Psalm 103:8-12; 130; Isaiah 59:1-4a; I John 1:9

# 1 Getting Started

## Housekeeping

Are there people absent from your group who need encouragement? Think of a way to encourage them. Give them a call, plan to visit them, or make a quick card and have everyone sign it. Make necessary announcements and introductions as needed.

## Icebreaker

Offer a wrapped gift (something small and inexpensive) to everyone who is willing to show the rest of the group the contents of his or her wallet. One at a time, ask each person to show and comment on the contents of his or her wallet. (It's surprising how much a wallet can reveal!)

Then talk briefly about how easy or difficult it was to accept the gift and share "secrets."

## Opening

Spend a few minutes worshiping God with music. As a group sing a song that deals with salvation. One of the songs you might consider is "I Am the Resurrection."

# 3 Bible Study

### Leadership Tip

Remember to set aside time for rest and refreshment in the presence of God. Try cancelling one of your activities this week and spend this time resting. Don't answer the phone. Don't work. Do something you enjoy, but do it alone with the Lord. Take a walk. Draw a picture. Relax, be still, and know that He is God. Remember, you are a human *being* not a human *doing*.

## Focus

Ask if any of your group members have ever been in a situation where they needed someone to "save" them. (This could include salvation from anything from a bad conversation to a physically dangerous situation.) Ask them to share how it felt to be in the situation, what they needed to do to get help, and how it felt to be rescued. Then ask several people to share their response to the question regarding how repentance, regret, and confession are connected (from the "Scripture Discovery" section of their journals).

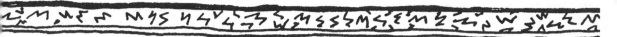

 ## Dig In

Ask someone to read Psalm 130. Then ask the following questions:

• This psalm can be divided into sections based on the psalmist's audience. Divide the psalm. (The three sections are as follows: verses 1-4; verses 5 and 6; and verses 7 and 8.) Who is the psalmist addressing in each section?

• Why do you think the psalmist cries out to the Lord in verse 1?

• What do we learn about God in verses 1-4?

• Look at verse 4. Why do you think fear is a response to God's forgiveness?

• What is the psalmist doing about his condition?

• Describe the duties of a watchman. How might a watchman be feeling as morning approaches? What does the coming of morning result in for the watchman?

• Do you think the Lord came to the waiting psalmist? Why or why not? Support your answer from the text.

• Look at verses 7 and 8. Why should Israel put its hope in the Lord?

• What does the psalmist proclaim in verse 8? Does he have a basis for this proclamation? Explain.

## Reflect and Respond

Ask everyone to close his or her eyes. Reread Psalm 130. Then have group members sit in a circle. Read Isaiah 59:1-4a. Pass a container of mud around the circle. Have each person rub mud on the back of his or her hand to symbolize sinfulness. Then read I John 1:9 and have a short time of silent confession. Finally, read Psalm 103:8-12. In response, pass around a clean, damp, white cloth, having each person rub off the mud on the hand of the person sitting next to him or her until each person's hand is clean. Then hold up the cloth and remind group members that Christ has taken the stain of our sin upon Himself so that we might be clean. Praise Him for this.

# 3 Sharing and Prayer

Instead of sharing prayer requests and praises, go directly into a time of group prayer. As you pray, you will be sharing and praising. Concentrate on what others are saying, agreeing with them and praying silently for them as they pray aloud.

## INSIDE INSIGHTS

■ Psalm 130 is thought by some to have been written when the author was in captivity. It is the sixth of seven penitential psalms. The other penitential psalms include Psalms 6, 32, 38, 51, 102, and 143.

■ In Bible times, watchtowers were built to protect pastures from thieves. They were also built into the defenseworks of larger cities. Watchmen in the watchtowers were on the alert for hostile action against the city. They were also there to give word to the king of any person approaching the city wall. In time of hostility, the dangers of the night were especially feared and the watchmen looked forward to the break of day. (See Isaiah 21:11, 12; II Samuel 18:24-27; II Kings 9:17-20.)

# WEEK 10 The Faith Factor

**Theme:** Our faith is shown through our actions.

**Scripture:** Genesis 15:6; 22:1-19; Joshua 2:1-21; Ephesians 2:8-10; James 2:14-26

# 1 Getting Started

## Housekeeping

Use this time to make any necessary announcements regarding the group—changes in meeting time, location, etc. You may also want to spend some time evaluating the study thus far.

## Icebreaker

Have group members pair off. Give each pair a piece of paper and a pencil. Ask the members of each pair to determine who will be the "eyes" and who will be the "artist." Have the "eyes" and the "artist" sit back to back, facing in opposite directions (with all the "eyes" facing the same direction). Tape a simple drawing to the wall. It should not be something easy to describe, but rather something abstract. The "eyes" must then instruct the "artist" what to draw. Allow no more than three minutes to complete the drawings. At the conclusion, compare all of the drawings to determine a winner.

## Opening

Read the following prayer: "**Almighty and everlasting God, who in the Paschal mystery hast established the new covenant of reconciliation: Grant that all who have been reborn into the fellowship of Christ's Body may show forth in their lives what they profess by their faith; through the same Jesus Christ our Lord, who liveth and reigneth with thee and the Holy Spirit, one God, for ever and ever. Amen.**"

Discuss the meaning of this prayer and then pray it in unison. (Note: "Paschal" describes something "of or pertaining to Passover or Easter." Jesus Christ has been referred to as our Paschal Lamb.)

# 2 Bible Study

### Leadership Tip

The founding fathers of the United States knew that all leaders need some checks and balances, some accountability in their leadership role. Ask someone you trust and respect to be your accountability partner. Be honest and share your struggles with him or her. Pray together, jotting down what you pray about in a journal so that you can see how God is working. It is best to have an accountability partner of the same sex.

## Focus

Most likely, everyone in your group has experienced or knows someone who has experienced a time when a person's actions were not sync with his or her words. Write the following phrases on a large piece of paper; then ask the questions that follow.

"Do what I say, not what I do."

"Your actions speak so loud that I can't hear what you're saying."

**Who do these sayings bring to mind? Share how a discrepancy between words and deeds has affected you.**

Allow time for brief discussion (some of your group members may have strong feelings about people who say one thing but do another), then move on to the "Dig In" section of the session.

## Dig In

Read James 2:14-26. Then ask the following questions:

• In verse 14, James poses some tough questions. How would you answer them?

• In the next few verses, James illustrates his point. How do you react to this story? Can you identify with either of the characters? How would you illustrate verse 17?

• What is faith? Explain the relationship between faith and deeds.

• According to James, how significant is belief in God? Explain.

• James gives examples from the Old Testament to support his point. Read the stories of Abraham (Genesis 15:6; 22:1-19) and Rahab (Joshua 2:1-21). What do these two stories and individuals have in common? How do they differ?

• Would Abraham have offered Isaac on the altar if he did not possess faith? Does faith come from deeds or are deeds an outworking of faith? Explain.

• Explain the phrases "credited to him as righteousness" (James 2:23) and "considered righteous" (verses 21 and 25).

• James summarizes this entire section with a metaphor in verse 26. What is your understanding of this metaphor?

Read Ephesians 2:8-10. Then ask the following question:

• Does James contradict Paul's teaching? Explain.

## Reflect and Respond

On a large piece of paper or chalkboard write the following George MacDonald quote from the "Scripture Discovery" section of the *Search of the Soul Journal*: "What a man believes is the thing he does, not the thing he thinks."

Ask for some reactions to this quote. See whether group members agree or disagree with it. Then take several minutes to discuss ways that a person might act out his or her faith.

## INSIDE INSIGHTS

■ In James 2:20, the word translated "useless" is *argos*, which means elsewhere, "not working," or "idle." Jesus used it to describe workers who had not been hired for the day (Matthew 20:3, 6). James's choice of the word here creates a pointed play on words: "Faith that has no works does not work!"

■ We must recognize that Paul's "faith" in Ephesians 2:8-10 and James' "faith alone" in James 2:14-26 are different concepts. Paul has a strongly dynamic concept of faith, by which the believer is intimately united with Christ, his or her Lord, and which results in a commitment of obedience to that Lord. Obedience results from faith (Romans 1:5; I Thessalonians 1:3) and expresses itself through love (Galatians 5:6). While James's basic concept of faith may not be entirely different from this, he speaks throughout verses 14-26 of a "faith" that certain people claim to have (verse 14). This "faith" is a matter of speech without action (verses 15 and 16)—verbal profession without trust and commitment (verses 18 and 19). James is talking about a false faith.

# 3 Sharing and Prayer

Have group members form pairs. Encourage them to exchange some thoughts on faith and doubt from the "Reflection" section in their journals.

Have your group members remain with their discussion partners to pray for each other.

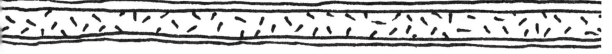

# UNIT Three

# The End of the Search, The Beginning of a Journey

Summer camp brings back fond memories for many people. A week away from home, free of parents, on your own for perhaps the first time. A week during which you could make your own decisions—for good or bad—and often a week when you first felt the full effect of making your own decisions.

But you weren't on your own entirely. There were plenty of other campers to share in your adventures. There were counselors to help you learn and grow. And your parents equipped you well before you left, making sure that you had a sleeping bag and plenty of clean underwear.

In many ways, the Christian life is not unlike that week at summer camp. There are fellow sojourners we can share and learn with; older, more experienced Christians who offer guidance and wisdom; and most importantly, God's equipping us for the journey. He did not promise that the journey would be easy, but He has promised to be with us and to support us the entire length of our journey.

In this unit, we will take a look at the beginning of that journey and just how God can help us along its path.

*About the author: Lorraine Mulligan Davis did her undergraduate work at Houghton College in New York and her graduate work at The College of William and Mary in Virginia. The author of hundreds of articles and stories, Lorraine has been the editor of two Christian magazines, a book and curriculum writer, and a costumed interpreter at a living history museum village. She lives in Wheaton, Illinois, with her husband, Scott, and two children.*

# Under New Ownership

**Theme:** Choosing to serve Christ, rather than sin, is an ongoing process in a Christian's life.

**Scripture:** Luke 6:43-49; Romans 6:12-23; Hebrews 11:23-29, 39, 40

# 1 Getting Started

## Housekeeping

Welcome new people to the group, and make any necessary announcements.

## Icebreaker

Have each person in the group think of his or her favorite boss, whether at a paid job or a volunteer job. Then show the group a stack of small, construction-paper squares in all of the primary colors. Have each person choose one piece of paper to tear into a shape that represents the

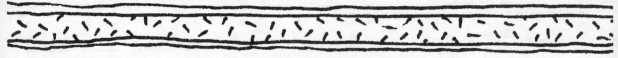

job held while working for that favorite boss. (You might want to show an example, such as a yellow crescent moon to indicate a night job at McDonald's, a square of green fringe to inidcate a job cutting lawns, a rolled-up white square to indicate delivering papers, etc.) Then have group members share their paper creations and explain what it was that they liked about their bosses.

## Opening

Say: **Maybe your favorite boss was a Christian. Maybe not. But was there anything about him or her that reminds you of Christ? If so, explain.**

After several group members have shared, pray together, asking God to open your eyes in the next few weeks to see more of who Christ really is, so that we can appreciate Him more fully.

# 2 Bible Study

## Focus

Say: **In our individualistic, democratic society, we're taught that true freedom includes being your own boss. But the introduction to Unit Three in our journals shows that it's essential to submit to a higher authority.** Ask someone to read the unit introduction on pages 92 and 93 of the journal. The introduction is reprinted here in its entirety.

Japan is a country of kite connoisseurs. The Japanese have taken the fine art of kite making to, er, new heights. Perhaps most exciting are the kite fights they stage. That's when contestants try to cut each other's kite strings with their own glass-coated lines.

When a kite's line is cut, what do you think happens? The kite doesn't sail off like a runaway helium balloon. It plummets to the ground. A kite needs constant tension on the string to maintain its flight.

In that way, humans are like kites. We need someone to hold the string on

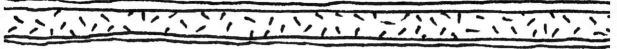

our lives. Once we're set free from Satan's powerful hold, we need Christ to take over! And what a difference there will be! Christ made us and knows the hazards unique to us—as well as how to bring out our fullest potential. With Christ in charge, we can really soar!

## Dig In

Ask someone to read Romans 6:12-23. Then ask the following questions:

• We studied this passage in our journals this week in the "Reflection" section on page 95. What are your observations about this passage?

• What is the result of being a slave to sin?

• What is the reward of being a slave to obedience to God?

The long-range rewards of obedience are clearly better. Yet millions of people have heard the claims of Christianity and have chosen the other alternative. Perhaps a glimpse into Moses' life will shed some light here.

Ask someone to read Hebrews 11:23-29. If you think some of your group members might not know Moses' story, share the information in "Inside Insights" on pages 84 and 85.

• What were the advantages of a life as one of Egypt's ruling family?

• Why did Moses choose to side with God's people instead?

Give each person in the group a piece of scrap paper. Then look together at the job descriptions on page 95 in the journal. On the scrap paper, fill out Moses' job description using the journal chart.

• By what criteria would a "slave to Satan" rate Moses' life? How did he measure up?

• By what criteria would a "slave to Christ" rate Moses' life? How did he measure up?

• Moses never got to live in the promised land. What insight does Hebrews 11:39, 40 shed on his real reward?

# INSIDE INSIGHTS

■ Throughout the years, Jesus Christ has been honored with countless names. Some of these names include "Lord of Lords," "Master," "King of Kings," "Counselor," "Captain of Our Salvation," "Defender," "Head," "Judge," "Majesty," "Protector," "Shepherd," "Sovereign," "Teacher," and "Prince of Peace."

■ Moses was born during a time when the Hebrew people were enslaved to the pharaoh of Egypt. They had been welcomed into Egypt when a Hebrew named Joseph was the pharaoh's second in command. Following God's orders, Joseph had carried out a plan that kept the whole world from starvation during a seven-year famine. The grateful pharaoh had insisted that Joseph invite his father and entire family to live in Egypt. But eventually Joseph and his generation died. The new ruler did not know Joseph. The Hebrews were made slaves and were persecuted because the Egyptians grew fearful of their increased power and prosperity.

Moses was born during a time when all Hebrew baby boys were supposed to be killed. When his mother couldn't hide him any longer, she placed him in a watertight basket near the banks of the Nile. Pharaoh's own daughter found him, and Moses was raised as her son. When Moses was forty years old, he took his first step to avenge his people by killing an Egyptian

*(continued on next page)*

# Reflect and Respond

Say: **Throughout Jesus' life, He was very clear regarding what it meant to make Him Lord. This week we saw that through His explanation in Luke 6:43-49.**

Ask group members to share their insights into these two parables. This would be a good time for group members to share any struggles they are having either digging "the solid foundation" or withstanding "the floods." Write down any struggles that are shared and any suggestions group members offer.

### Leadership Tip

When a group member shares a problem or loss, it is not your job to explain it or make things perfect. But here are some things you *can* say with confidence:

1. I'm so sorry.

2. If you want to talk, I will listen.

3. God cares about you.

4. Is there any way I can help?

# 3 Sharing and Prayer

Suggest that group members write down some struggles to pray for now and throughout the week.

Close with a time of worship. Have group members pool all of the names for Christ symbolizing His lordship that they recorded in the "Response" section of their journals. Then have group members pray, thanking Jesus that He is willing to have us call Him our "Lord of Lords," "Master," "King of Kings," etc. Close by singing "He Is Lord" together.

## INSIDE INSIGHTS

(continued from preceding page)

who was hurting a Hebrew slave. But when his action became known, he ran away to the wilderness. After Moses spent forty years as a nomad, God commanded him to return to Egypt as His spokesman.

Moses did return. At first, the Hebrews cheered him on. But when things seemed to get worse rather than better, they complained even louder than they had praised God. However, after ten plagues sent from God to destroy the ten "gods" of Egypt, Pharaoh finally urged the Hebrews to leave Egypt.

The emancipated Hebrew slaves turned out to be a difficult group to lead. They repeatedly disobeyed, rebelled, complained, and forgot God. What could have been a short journey to their new land became forty years of learning and relearning how to be God's people. Moses was not perfect, but he humbly depended on God and tried to obey God's commands. Though Moses never got the chance to live in the promised land, Exodus 33:11 tells us, "The Lord would speak to Moses face to face, as a man speaks with his friend."

# WEEK 12 Giver of Grace

**Theme:** Appreciating our freedom in Christ frees us to serve God and others in love.

**Scripture:** Psalm 56:12, 13; Romans 12:1-21; Galatians 5:1-15

# 1 Getting Started

## Housekeeping

Welcome everyone to the study. If there are any new people, make introductions and then make sure that they have what they need to participate. Briefly make any necessary announcements; then move on to the study.

## Icebreaker

Remember Mary Poppins's measuring tape? It measured Jane as "Rather Inclined to Giggle, Doesn't Put Things Away"; Michael as "Extremely Stubborn and Suspicious"; and Mary Poppins as "Practically Perfect in Every Way."

Have your group members draw themselves standing next to a ruler and apply Mary Poppins's measuring tape to themselves. They could do this on scrap paper or on an uncluttered place in their journals. Instead of numbers, have them write the standards that the world measures them by. Then have them contrast that to what God's measurement would be.

## Opening

Explain: **Today we'll be studying our privileges in Christ. Let's begin by singing, "Father, I Adore You."** You might also choose another song of thanksgiving. Open the session with prayer.

# 2 Bible Study

## Focus

Say: **Salvation is the most amazing gift imaginable—or unimaginable. After thousands of year of preparation, the God of the Universe arrived on Planet Earth to take upon Himself the sins of the world. The result was the free gift of salvation. And it truly is free— no strings attached. You can rely on Him for your salvation, not because of your special ability to follow the rules, but because Jesus Christ died in your place. When God looks at you, He sees Jesus Christ's righteousness— not your own. You are a child of God with full rights and privileges.**

**Some people receive this gift of salvation just seconds before they die—and are ushered into heaven right away. But it doesn't happen that way for most people. Many people have years left on Earth before they will enter heaven. Regardless, once we've accepted the gift of salvation, we've been declared blameless by God. We're in a privileged position, something like the boss's kid mentioned on page 102 in the journal—or like royalty. So how should our privileged position affect the rest of our lives?**

### Leadership Tip

Be sensitive to any "boss's kids" who might be present. Ask if any of your group members work for their families' businesses. Have them share any insights they might have on the topic. For instance:

• What are the special demands or privileges of the job?

• How are they treated by employees who are not part of the family?

 **Dig In**

Have someone read Galatians 5:1-15. Then ask the following questions:

• What is freedom in Christ?

• What is the yoke of slavery?

• What religious practices were some people trying to tack on to the process of salvation by faith? Why do you suppose they were doing that?

Have someone reread Galatians 5:13, 14: "You, my brothers, were called to be free. But do not use your freedom to indulge the sinful nature; rather, serve one another in love. The entire law is summed up in a single command: 'Love your neighbor as yourself.' "

 Say: Look back at Psalm 56:12, 13 in the "Reflection" section of your journals. The psalmist talks about offering God thank offerings. The apostle Paul gets more specific.

Ask someone to read Romans 12:1-21. Then ask the following questions:

• How does Paul describe a person who has become a living sacrifice?

• What must be renewed in order for a person to stop conforming to the pattern of this world? How do you think this happens?

• How is a person supposed to form an estimation of himself or herself?

• What do you think it means that you should think of yourself "in accordance with the measure of faith God has given you" (verse 3)?

• When estimating people's accomplishments, do you use the measurement of their God-given faith? Why do you think God does?

• What light does Galatians 5:6 shed on this question?

• The psalmist's "thank offerings" foreshadows Paul's "living sacrifices." If you were going to give God such a gift, what would it be?

## Reflect and Respond

Give group members time to fine-tune the thank-you notes they wrote to God in the "Response" section on page 107 of their journals.

Point out that many times our greatest weaknesses are simply the flip side of our greatest God-given strengths. (For example, a person who works great with people may have a hard time finishing important tasks that must be done alone; a person who thrives on meeting the needs of others may not know when to say no.)

Ask for volunteers willing to share their notes. In doing so, they can ask for accountability in carrying out their promises to God.

# 3 Sharing and Prayer

Give group members time to share what they got out of this study, including any questions or concerns they have. Then have a time of sharing about how the past week went. Last week, you studied serving Jesus Christ as Lord. Ask if anyone has a

## INSIDE INSIGHTS

■ Judaizers were Jews who entered the church who believed that certain ceremonial practices from the Old Testament were still binding. Speaking up after Paul had left Galatia, they questioned Paul's authority, insisting that he was not a "true apostle" and was trying to ingratiate himself with the Galatians by making the Christian life look easy. Throughout the centuries and right up to the present, people have tried to add their own pet religious laws and customs as requirements for salvation. They are acting in the spirit of the Judaizers.

Through Christ, we don't have to live in the shadow of other people's expectations for us. We mainly have to account to God. Notice that Romans 12:3 does not say that you are to avoid thinking highly of yourself. The danger is in thinking of yourself "more highly than you ought." Many people secretly believe that they will find nothing but correction when they approach God through Scripture. However, I John 3:19, 20 points out that when "our hearts condemn us. . . . God is greater than our hearts, and he knows everything." We will find comfort and reassurance as well as correction in God's Word. If any of your group members seem to hold a faulty view of God and His Word, try to address this.

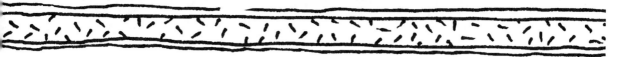

victory to share or a struggle that he or she would like help overcoming. Emphasize the importance of keeping up with the journals and in encouraging each other throughout the week. (Make sure that everyone has a list of group members' names and phone numbers.)

Leave plenty of time to praise God for His gift of salvation and to pray for any requests. Then close with a song like "Thank You, Lord."

### For next week:

Before you begin your personal journal entry, make an enlarged photocopy of the "Narrow Way" drawing on page 111 of the journal to fill out as a group at your next meeting.

Locate two mirrors. Their use is explained in the Leadership Tip on page 95.

Make copies of a list of group members' names, addresses, and phone numbers to distribute next week.

# No One Said It Would Be Easy

**Theme:** The Christian life involves struggle and growth.

**Scripture:** Romans 7:1-25; Philippians 3:4-6, 12-14; I Timothy 1:15

# 1 Getting Started

## Housekeeping

Welcome any newcomers to the group and be sure to introduce them to everyone else in the group. Then make any necessary announcements.

## Icebreaker

One Step Forward . . .

Have group members stand in a line so that there's plenty of room in front of them and behind them. Then say: **I'm going to ask each of you to take a step forward. The person who ends up furthest forward wins.** Display a small treat that will be the prize. Have group members take a step forward.

After you've noted everyone's position, say: **By the way, the name of this game is "One Step Forward, Two Steps Back." So each of you must take two backward steps that are the same length as the step you just took.** Unless someone cheats, the person who had done the worst to begin with will end up winning the treat.

## Opening

Say: **Sometimes the Christian life seems just like the game we just played—one step forward, two steps back. As hard as we try, Satan and our own evil natures team up against us. It's important to remember that even when it's two against one, God is greater.**

Sing a song like "My God Is So Great, So Strong, and So Mighty." Pray for understanding of the truths God will bring to light in your study.

# 2 Bible Study

## Focus

Use the "Reflection" section on page 111 of the journal to begin this study. Display an enlarged photocopy of the Narrow Way illustration. (If you did not lead last week's study or did not know that you would need this large, blank copy, then make one copy and white out or cover your own answers before you make the enlargement.)

Ask people to share some of the labels they came up with. If you think your group members might not share their responses, have some hypothetical labels ready to write in.

Say: **I thought Jesus said, "Come to me, all you who are weary and burdened, and I will give you rest. Take my yoke upon you and learn from me, for I am gentle and humble in heart, and you will find rest for your souls. For my yoke is easy and my burden is light" (Matthew 11:28-30). Did you expect to be battling these problems after having Jesus Christ living in you? Why or why not?**

94

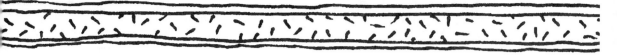

 ## Dig In

Read Romans 7:1-13. Then ask the following questions:

• **What was the original purpose of the law?**

(The original purpose was not to create right and wrong, but to alert people to what right and wrong was and to God's standard of life—perfection.)

• **Why was it impossible for the law to save anyone?**

(No one could fulfill the law.)

• **Once a person has realized his or her need for a Savior and accepted Jesus' gift of redemption, what place does the law have in that person's life?**

(The law shows us the character of a holy God and the guidelines He expects in behavior.)

Have someone read Romans 7:14-25. Then ask the following questions:

• **What was Paul's ongoing struggle? Why was this a struggle for him?**

Have someone read Philippians 3:4-6 and I Timothy 1:15. The ask the following question:

• **Why do you think Paul could say both things about himself?**

(Even Paul's meticulous righteousness was not good enough in comparison to God's holy standard. The more you understand holiness, the more you see your own sinfulness.)

*Leadership Tip*

The following object lesson might explain Paul's seeming contradictions. Show the group two small mirrors, one that is clean and one that you have made dirty, perhaps with dish soap mixed with dirt. Pass the mirrors around, letting group members notice their reflections in each mirror.

Sometimes people who are sensitive to God—who see themselves clearly in the mirror—will see more imperfections in their lives. Other people have such a foggy view of themselves that they can live cheerfully with glaring faults.

# INSIDE INSIGHTS

■ If you read only Romans 7:14-25, you'd think the writer was a weak-willed loser. That was far from the case! Paul has an amazing story. The apostle Paul (or Saul, as he was called among the Jews) typified himself as a "Pharisee of the Pharisees." Before he met Christ, he followed the Jewish law meticulously, but he put his trust in his own righteousness, not the Messiah that God had promised to provide. Paul persecuted the new church, helping those who stoned Stephen and dragging Christians from their homes and throwing them in prison.

On his way to the city of Damascus to persecute converts there, Paul was blinded by a light from heaven. Jesus Christ spoke to him there and changed his life forever. Paul became a tireless disciple of Christ—just as he had been a tireless antagonist. He came to understand that his righteousness could not be based on following the Jewish law and all of the extra rules the Pharisees emphasized. His righteousness was based on faith alone in Jesus' death on the cross.

*(continued on next page)*

No matter if Paul's sins were large or small, they were painfully apparent to him! In this way, the apostle Paul, writer of much of the New Testament, was not very different from us!

Say: **We shared some of our own struggles a few minutes ago. Next week's study will concentrate on how, with God's help, we can tackle our habitual sins and weaknesses in a systematic way. But now we're going to talk about what to do with the frustration and discouragement that accompanies our all-too-human failures.**

 Have group members read the quote from *Feeling Good* in the "Reaction" section of the journal on page 114. Then ask: **What do you think we can learn from this quote when our sins and weaknesses threaten to overwhelm us?**

Point out that Paul echoed this feeling when he wrote Philippians 3:12-14. Read this passage aloud. Then ask the following question:

• **It's been said that Satan doesn't need to lead us into terrible sin. It's enough to lead us into the paralysis of discouragement. He does a lot of his damage with one little word— "Again?"! How could we respond in a case like that?**

One way to fight Satan at his own game is to do this: Greet each memory of past sin with the statement, "And that's one more reason to give Jesus my life. He's earned it!" If Satan's reminders cause you to love God more, he'll stop reminding you.

 ## Reflect and Respond

Ask: **Would these methods help you fight discouragement? Why or why not?**

Try to identify the reasons group members sometimes lose the battle with discouragement. See if your group can brainstorm solutions to the problem. Solutions might include forming encouragement partners, with one person helping another person keep things in perspective and set reasonable goals for overcoming ingrained problems.

Suggest that group members read, meditate on, and even memorize the following verses if they struggle in the areas that are listed:

• Don't feel forgiven—I John 1:9; Psalm 103:12

• Nagging regret—I Thessalonians 5:18; Romans 8:28, 29

• When they've sinned *again*— Romans 7:21–8:4; Luke 7:47; James 4:6b

*(continued from preceding page)*

Yet it took time for the church to accept him as a leader. He spent some years in Arabia while he prepared for ministry. Tradition has it that Paul had an unsightly eye disorder that made him less than attractive. Even so, he started many churches throughout the Roman world. Thirteen of the letters he wrote to those churches and individuals have become a large part of the New Testament. He suffered all of the injustices he had once committed against the Christians, including death for his faith.

*Leadership Tip*

Be cautious, too, not to let group members get the impression that problems should be ignored. Paul's suggestion about "forgetting what is behind" has been greatly abused! If, in next week's meeting, someone expresses bewilderment as to what the source of his or her repetitive failure is or how to correct it, that person might benefit from talking to your group's leader, the pastor, a strong Christian that the person trusts and admires, or a Christian counselor.

# 3 Sharing and Prayer

Give group members time for further sharing, both from their journals and from their experiences this week. Follow up on last week's prayer concerns, and share new ones. Pray together. Then close by singing a worshipful hymn or chorus such as "I'm Forever Grateful."

*For next week:*

Ask people who have access to Bible concordances to bring them.

# You're Not Alone!

**Theme:** God is our helpmate in overcoming temptation.

**Scripture:** Psalm 119:9-16; Luke 4:1-13

# 1 Getting Started

## Housekeeping

Welcome any newcomers to the group, making sure to introduce them to everyone else in the group. Then make any necessary announcements.

## Icebreaker

### The Paper Bag Game

On slips of paper, write famous pairs such as the following: Sherlock Holmes/Dr. Watson, Batman/Robin, Ben/Jerry, Starsky/Hutch, Ernie/Bert, Hamlet/Horatio, Butch Cassidy/The Sundance Kid, Tweedledee/Tweedledum, Stanley/Livingston, Chip/Dale, Simon/Garfunkel, Jonathan/David, Tootie/Muldoon, Snoopy/Woodstock, Hope/Crosby, Cagney/Lacey, Paul/Silas, Laurel/Hardy, Laverne/Shirley, Fred/Barney.

Place all of the slips in one paper bag. Divide the group into two teams. Have each team choose the first person to give the clues. Then hand the paper bag to one group. Someone should start counting out thirty seconds. Within that time, the clue giver will draw a slip and say whatever is needed to get the group to identify the twosome. The clue giver can say anything but the actual names. If it looks like a slip is too hard for the group, the person can drop that slip back into the bag and choose another. When the group guesses a slip, that paper is saved, another slip is drawn, and the group keeps playing until all thirty seconds are up.

After thirty seconds, the other team goes. For each new round, new people become the clue givers. Once all of the pairs have been guessed, each team counts up its collected papers to determine which team guessed the most. You might have a small treat for the winning team.

## Opening

Choose a song that expresses God's companionship and help, such as "There Is a Friend," "What a Friend We Have in Jesus," or "He Is Able."

For your opening prayer, suggest that group members each contribute one thought to finish the sentence, "Lord, what I especially appreciate about Your friendship is . . ."

# 2 Bible Study

## Focus

Say: **It doesn't take a master's degree in psychology to know that some of us enjoy being alone more than others do. Some of us draw strength from solitary moments. Others get their energy from being with a group or with a few good friends.**

Ask volunteers to share a description of the type of situation that would energize them. If they enjoy being with people, encourage them to share what it is about a group that excites them or gives them energy. If they tend to prefer solitude, encourage them to talk about what they like about being alone. You may also wish to point out and talk about the difference between being alone and being lonely.

 Ask group members to share some of their answers from the "Reflection" section on page 119. Have an account of your own ready.

## Dig In

Review what group members studied in the "Scripture Discovery" section on pages 120 and 121 of the journal.

Read Luke 4:1-13. Then ask the following questions:
• **What were the three ways Satan tempted Jesus?**
• **What made the temptations so appealing?**
• **In each case, how did Jesus combat Satan's suggestions?**

Read Psalm 119:9-16. Have group members share their answers to the chart ("What the writer promises to do"/"What he asks God to do") on page 121 in their journals.

Ask: **How does it make you feel to know that you don't have to face temptation alone?**

Point out that Scripture is one language the Holy Spirit uses to speak to us. But like any language, it must be learned! And learning comes with exposure.

Have someone read the Paul Little quote on page 123 of the journal.

Then ask: **What do you think spiritual power is? What effect would it have on the sins and weaknesses we listed in our journals last week?**

## Reflect and Respond

See how group members did in filling out page 122 in the "Reaction" section of their journals. Ask group members to share "The Challenge" they identified and the Scripture passages they chose to help them meet it. If some group members need help understanding the process, go through the following example. You could also take some time to brainstorm Scripture passages and related topics to look up in your concordances.

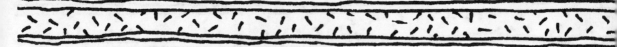

Here's an example of how to fill in "The Challenge."

• Review your list of sins or weaknesses. Choose one to start working on right now.

*The Challenge: Lying*

Related topics to look up in the concordance: truth, trustworthiness, falsehood.

*Scripture passages:*

1. Proverbs 19:5

2. Psalm 34:12, 13

3. Philippians 4:8

4. Proverbs 16:13

| *Especially Hard Situations* | *How I'll Anticipate/Overcome It* |
|---|---|
| • I lie when I think someone will think less of me for telling the truth or will try to hurt me.<br>• I lie when I'm afraid of the consequences. | • I could remind myself that God's opinion of me is most important.<br>• I could remind myself of the consequences of the lie itself, even if I get myself off the hook.<br>• I can assure myself that God can protect me. |

• **What could you do to make Scripture work for you?**

Give group members a moment of silence in which they can make plans with God about how they will spend quality time with Him.

If time allows, try to memorize a verse together so that group members understand the process of memorizing. "Inside Insights" gives steps for one way of memorizing.

# 3 Sharing and Prayer

Have a general time of sharing personal concerns and prayer requests. This would be a good time, too, to share any prayer requests concerning "The Challenge." Make sure to allow at least five to ten minutes for prayer.

## Leadership Tip

Some portions of the study are very personal. If you think your group members will have trouble sharing, you might contact one or two of them before the study to ask if they will think ahead about sharing with the group.

## INSIDE INSIGHTS

■ How to Memorize a Verse

1. Say the reference out loud while looking at it.

2. Say the first phrase out loud—three times while looking and two times without looking.

3. Say the next phrase out loud—three times while looking and two times without looking.

4. Combine the reference and both phrases, saying them out loud, one time looking and one time without looking.

5. Add more phrases in the same way.

6. Say the reference again at the end.

7. Repeat the process as often as possible.

Of course, difficult verses may need more repetitions. It sometimes helps, too, to write the verses on a piece of paper or tape-record verses to listen to while you do other things.

# What More Could You Ask For?

**Theme:** God has given us everything we need in order to live and grow in Him.

**Scripture:** John 14:15-20, 26-31; Acts 2:40-47; Romans 8; Galatians 5:22, 23; Ephesians 3:16-19

# 1 Getting Started

## Housekeeping

This is the last week in this study guide on searching for—and finding—God. Decide as a group if you would like to have a special meeting next week. It could be a meal, a dessert smorgasbord, or an ultimate make-your-own-pizzas/sundaes party. During the gathering, you could evaluate how the last fifteen meetings went and decide on a new study guide, such as *Who Am I? 15 Small Group Studies on Discovering Personal Worth*.

Welcome any guests, make sure everyone has the materials he or she needs, and make any necessary announcements.

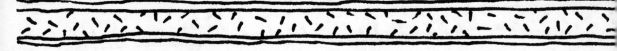

## Icebreaker

### Fill 'er Up

Place before the group a large tray with a piece of construction paper on top of it, a one-quart Mason jar filled with two-and-a-half cups of rice, and twenty-five whole walnuts. Instruct group members to do whatever they need to in order to fit the whole walnuts into the rice jar without breaking up the walnuts. Give them a few minutes to work on this.

*Solution*—If you try to stuff the walnuts into the jar of rice, the walnuts simply won't fit. But if you make the construction paper into a cone, pour the rice inside, then place all of the walnuts in the empty jar and pour the rice around the walnuts, it will work.

## Opening

Say: **Today we will be studying the Holy Spirit's work in our lives. Let's begin with a song honoring the Spirit.** Sing a song such as "Father, I Adore You," "There's a Sweet, Sweet Spirit in This Place," or "Every Time I Feel the Spirit." Then ask someone to open in prayer.

# 2 Bible Study

## Focus

Use the "Reflection" section on page 127 of the journal to begin the study.

Have group members share their diary entries in which they pretend they are a disciple writing down his initial reaction to the news that Jesus was going away.

As group members share, jot down the thoughts and emotions that surface. Then as a group, try to summarize the reasons Jesus' departure was such world-changing news.

## Dig In

Explain: **Before Jesus died on the cross, the disciples knew only two ways of life: life before Jesus came into their lives and life with Jesus beside them. They had no way to envision the third way of life that was about to happen—Jesus, through the presence of the Holy Spirit, living inside of them.**

Read John 14:15-20, 26-31. As you discuss the following questions, have group members refer to their notes in the "Scripture Discovery" section on pages 128 and 129 of their journals.

Explain that the conversation in this passage happened during the Last Supper, the Passover feast that Jesus and His disciples shared just before Jesus was arrested. Then ask the following questions:

• **How did Jesus describe the One He would send to take His place among them?**

• **Why would the world deny the Spirit's existence?**

• **What did Jesus promise that the Spirit would do for Christians?**

Jot down this last question and your group's answers on a large sheet of paper.

Then say: **Within days, Jesus was dead—and alive again! He appeared to the disciples for forty days (Acts 1:3) before He ascended into heaven, saying "I am going to send you what my Father has promised; but stay in the city until you have been clothed with power from on high" (Luke 24:49).**

On Pentecost, the Holy Spirit descended on the disciples like tongues of fire. Until Steven Spielberg makes the movie, we may never even glimpse an event like that day. The once-fearful Christians took to the streets, overflowing with words about Christ in languages they hadn't known before. They were so deliriously joyful that onlookers thought they were drunk! Acts 2 tells the story.

Ask someone to read Acts 2:40-47 aloud. Then ask the following questions:

• **How were the disciples changed people once the Holy Spirit entered their lives?**

• **What character qualities and abilities did the Holy Spirit bring out in the Christians?**

• **How were Jesus' promises fulfilled?**

Add this last question, and your group's answers, to the same paper you used earlier. Continue to look for comments to add to this sheet throughout the study.

Then say: **This week, in the "Scripture Discovery" section on pages 128 and 129 of the journal, you studied some ways in which the Holy Spirit helps us.**

Ask some group members to read Romans 8 aloud. Then ask the following questions:

• **What's your initial response to this chapter?**

• **How did you respond to the list on page 129?** Encourage several group members to offer their responses.

 ## Reflect and Respond

Go through the following questions:

• **What new truths did you learn about the Holy Spirit in this study?**

• **What kind of difference do you think He can make in your life?** For further help in answering this question, look to Galatians 5:22, 23 and Ephesians 3:16-19.

• **What would help you turn more "Lord, show me!" responses into "Thank you, Lord!" responses?**

• **The introductory game today was also an object lesson involving the Holy Spirit. Can anyone decipher the meaning?**

In it, the Christian is the jar, the walnuts are the Holy Spirit and His priorities, and the rice are all of the other things in the Christian's life. For them all to fit, the Holy Spirit and His priorities need to be in place first.

• **What are the Spirit's priorities?** Galatians 5:22, 23 and Ephesians 3:16-19 give examples.

• **What is your rice—those everyday desires, tasks, and responsibilities that could easily dominate your life?**

If you haven't already done so, consider forming encouragement partners that will help one another continue the good work they have begun during this series of studies. Right now the partners can brainstorm ways to become more open to the Spirit's work in their lives. If time allows, come back together to share once more in the large group.

# 3 Sharing and Prayer

As people share prayer requests today, have them include one praise to God for something He has taught them during this fifteen-week study.

After prayer time, close by reciting together Romans 8:31, 32, 38, 39, which appears on page 131 in the journal. Adjourn with another brief prayer of thanks to God.

### Leadership Tip

If group members need more guidance in how to open themselves up to the Spirit's work in their lives, you can offer these suggestions:

1. Accept Christ as Savior (explained in Week 9).

2. Memorize and meditate on Scripture (explained in Week 14).

## INSIDE INSIGHTS

■ Scripture treats the fruit of the Spirit as a unified whole—more like an apple-bananagrapefruit than apples, bananas, and grapefruit. Yet each quality has a very specific "flavor."

• Love—Being committed to someone, to sacrifice for him or her, to give him or her the benefit of the doubt, to hope for his or her best, to care.

• Joy—Having an exuberant disposition that comes from knowing that God is emphatically for us.

• Peace—Being content with who you are and who God is.

• Patience—Being able to wait for God's timing, especially when your own timetable is not being met.

• Kindness—Being willing to help others with a loving and sympathetic nature.

• Goodness—Being able to know and act on what is right and appropriate; being helpful toward others.

• Faithfulness—Being responsible for your behavior and reliable to follow through on what you have committed to do.

• Gentleness—Having a quiet, nature that comes from being filled with God's love.

• Self-control—Having the ability to confront sinful impulses and prevent them from becoming sinful actions; being disciplined.

on "The Challenge" (explained in Week 14) and use the sys-
other weaknesses on your list.

God with a servant's attitude. Then listen. He may bring to mind
an do. Or an opportunity (however tiny or commonplace) may
way to serve Him.

and claim Scripture passages that affirm a Christian's adoption by
throughout your day you can say, "How would a child of the King han-
his situation?"